Stuart Calvert

Woman's Missionary Union
Birmingham, Alabama

Woman's Missionary Union
P. O. Box 830010
Birmingham, AL 35283-0010

For more information, visit our Web site at www.wmu.com or call
1-800-968-7301.

Dewey Decimal Classification: 248.4
Subject Heading: CHRISTIAN LIFE

Unless otherwise indicated, Scripture quotations are from the Holy Bible, New
International Version (NIV). Copyright © 1973, 1978, 1984 International Bible
Society. Used by permission of Zondervan Bible Publishers.

Scripture quotations identified CEV are from *Contemporary English Version.*
Copyright © American Bible Society 1991. Used by permission.

Scripture quotations identified TEV are from the *Good News Bible,* Today's
English Version. Old Testament: © American Bible Society, 1976; New Testament: © American Bible Society, 1966, 1971, 1976.

Scripture quotations identified KJV are from the King James Version.

Scripture quotations identified NASB are taken from the NEW AMERI-
CAN STANDARD BIBLE®, © Copyright The Lockman Foundation 1960, 1962,
1963, 1968, 1971, 1972, 1973, 1975, 1977. Used by permission.

Scripture quotations identified RSV are from the *Revised Standard Version.*
Old Testament: Copyright 1952, by Division of Christian Education of the
National Council of the Churches of Christ in the United States of America;
New Testament: Copyright 1946, by Division of Christian Education of the
National Council of the Churches of Christ in the United States of America.

Design by Janell E. Young

ISBN: 1-56309-559-9
W023102•0302 •7.5M1

CONTENTS

INTRODUCTION

"Let the plan of the Holy One of Israel come, so we may know it" (Isa. 5:14).

Assembling jigsaw puzzles provides many fun-filled hours for our family. Gazing at the picture of our newest puzzle, "Tempting Sweets," was like lifting the lid on a box of assorted chocolates. Imaginatively we smelled the rich aroma of fudge brownies. We savored the smooth succulent chocolate-dipped strawberries. With our taste buds stimulated, we unsealed the box and emptied the contents onto the green top of the game table. Someone sighed, "This is a puzzle to puzzle over," meaning concentration and cooperation would be necessary to connect the pieces. We expressed bewilderment over where to begin among the possibilities. We agreed that working together was less overwhelming than solving the puzzle alone.

The scattered pieces of "Tempting Sweets" did not reveal the complete picture. Searching the illustration on the box was the only way to know the design. We began immediately placing aside malt balls that at some point would connect with cocoa dusted crunchies. The more we looked at the picture, the more enthusiastic we became. The plan excited us.

God's Plan . . . My Part: The words *plan* and *part* are so familiar to us that we might miss the nuances in their meanings. Notice how the definitions of *plan* connect with Scriptures about God's plan.

A plan is an intention that has been worked out beforehand: "Having been predestined according to the plan of him who works out everything in conformity with the purpose of His will" (Eph. 1:11).

A plan proposes a way of doing something: Jesus defined God's plan, "For the Son of Man came to seek and to save what was lost" (Luke 10:10) so "that you may believe that Jesus is the Christ, the Son of God; and that believing you may have life in His name" (John 20:31).

A plan offers projects to achieve important enterprises, ventures, or tasks. God's plan is designed with a worldwide scope: "He told them, 'This is what is written: The Christ will suffer and rise from the dead on the third day, and repentance and forgiveness of sins will be preached in his name to all nations, beginning at Jerusalem'" (Luke 24:46–47).

God's plan is trustworthy: "The Lord almighty has sworn, 'Surely, as I have planned, so it will be, and as I have purposed, so it will stand'" (Isa. 14:24).

Consider the word *part*. *Part* is an impromptu, casual word. Offhandedly we say take *part; part* company; *part*-time; spare *parts*; *parts* of a puzzle.

Part also is essential to complete the whole. *Part* shares in the action. Paul's words to the Colossians explained his part in their ministry: "I want you to know how much I am struggling for you and for those at Laodicea, and for all who have not met me personally. My purpose is that they may be encouraged in heart and united in love" (Col. 2:1–2).

John Powell, author of *He Touched Me,* explained how imagination is one channel of communication from

God. He can speak to us through mental pictures. Imagination is the ability to create new mental images or to combine old ideas in new forms. Throughout *God's Plan . . . My Part,* agree to lend me your imagination.

God's Plan . . . My Part is presented in a puzzle format. Imagine a puzzle in the shape of a globe with the shadow of the Cross hovering over the continents.

Once I put together a puzzle entitled "Sunrise over the Pond." The scene was an eighteenth-century parlor where an elegantly dressed woman leaned over a pedestaled table assembling a puzzle. Her puzzle contained 16 of the larger puzzle's 500 pieces. The picture of her small puzzle, "Sunrise over the Pond," gradually appeared as I placed the pieces in the larger—a puzzle within a puzzle.

In *God's Plan . . . My Part,* Paul's part and my part are personal puzzle clusters within the larger globe puzzle. Each chapter contains the following sections:

• Puzzle Piece designates the biblical topic. The Bible is our word picture guide. The content describes how God fulfilled His plan through Jesus and others, like Paul.

• My Part is an introspective section. Your life's experiences form a cluster within God's plan. From your memory and present lifestyle, you can explain the way God is fulfilling His purpose for you (Psalm 138:8).

Although our circumstances differ from Paul's and from one another, our devotion to God's plan—to seek and to save the lost—is the same.

• Part and Parcel. From its Latin root, *parcel* means particular. Each of us is part and parcel—precise, necessary to God's plan. The Part and Parcel sections contain testimonies of both biblical and present-day people whose lives illustrate their part in God's plan.

In the first century, Paul was part and parcel of God's plan to preach to the Gentiles by crossing social and

4

religious barriers. Certainly Paul's faithful work, uncon-
ditional love, and deep suffering are worthy standards to
strive for or to meet in our own way. Yet Paul was only
one influential part in God's plan.

My part in God's plan is not an option. It is a divine
imperative: "You did not choose me, but I chose you and
appointed you to go and bear fruit—fruit that will last"
(John 15:16).

1

GOD'S PLAN *To Seek and to Save the Lost*

MY PART *To Witness*

"God presented him as a sacrifice of atonement, through faith in his blood" (Rom. 3:25).

Preparation for assembling the "Tempting Sweets" puzzle required rearranging 1,000 shapes to reveal bits and snippets of a pattern. As we spread out the pieces, we placed to one side the smooth-edged shapes to form a border. Without a boundary to form a puzzle the individual parts disconnect.

PUZZLE PIECE
Imagine a Globe Puzzle

The border of "God's Plan . . . My Part" is a dramatic design. Imagine how a calligrapher, with flowing strokes of crimson ink, surrounded the puzzle with: "For God so loved the world that he gave his one and only Son, that whoever believes in him shall not perish but have eternal life" (John 3:16).

Without a secure border, the pieces in life's puzzle will never fit together. When people trust the counterfeit promises of secular whims and false religions, life's puzzle becomes a jumble of irrelevant pieces. When we trust Jesus Christ as Savior, God keeps watch over life's cluster of pieces in this life and through eternity. Jesus said that He would not lose one person given to Him by the Father (John 6:39; 17:12). We rest secure in His promise.

PUZZLE PIECE
Imagine the Cross

For Paul (formerly Saul), the center of God's plan to seek and to save the lost was the Cross. Paul insisted, "We preach Christ crucified" (1 Cor. 1:23). To the Galatians, he wrote, "May I never boast except in the cross of our Lord Jesus Christ" (Gal. 6:14).

Four-year-old Taylor tore a cross shape from a scrap of paper. The bottom of the cross was wide. One side of the crosspiece was narrow; the other wide. On the narrow pointed top, above the crooked crosspiece, Taylor drew a stick figure of Jesus. On His slender hand was a pinpoint of red.

Pointing to the red dot, I asked, "Taylor, what is this?" Acquiring a serious pose, she answered, "It's blood." She thought a minute and continued, "GG, I think it drips on anybody who stands under it."

Oh yes! Not just drips of blood, Savior, but deluge me with an overwhelming rush. Thank You, Father, for the cleansing flood—the blood of Jesus.

Only the blood of Jesus can redeem.

Only His sacrifice can atone for sin.

Only His death can give us life.

Only His righteousness can justify us as not guilty.

Because of His resurrection from the grave and His

ascension to His Father, we enjoy the Holy Spirit, Christ's presence.

We rely on Christ's intercession.

We trust His daily guidance.

We possess eternal life.

Jesus' sacrifice is our incentive to accomplish our part in God's plan.

PUZZLE PIECE
Imagine a Manger and a Swirl of Matter

Later Taylor and I continued the conversation about Jesus and the Cross. Pointing to the stick figure, Taylor said, "He used to be a baby. He had a bed in a barn." Taylor could not comprehend elusive thoughts about God before time—yet.

Audibly I whispered, "And before His bed in the barn, He was with God."

Just before Taylor darted off, I noticed a quizzical wrinkle on her brow. A quizzical wrinkle describes my soul when I try to grasp the incomprehensible reality that before time God initiated a meticulous plan to seek and to save the lost.

• **God decided the plan before the creation of the world. The plan was not an afterthought:**
"He was chosen before the creation of the world, but was revealed in these last times for your sake" (1 Peter. 1:20).

"This grace was given us in Christ Jesus before the beginning of time" (2 Tim. 1:9).

• **God's plan was predetermined.**
"In him we were also chosen, having been predestined according to the plan of him who works out everything in conformity with the purpose of his will" (Eph. 1:11).

• **God revealed His plan through history.**
"It is written in Isaiah the prophet: 'I will send my messenger ahead of you, who will prepare your way—a voice of one calling in the desert, prepare the way for the Lord, make straight paths for him" (Mark 1:2–3).

• **God described the Messiah.** Isaiah 53 is an astounding, majestic prophecy that God would save the world through a sinless, Suffering Servant.

• **God's intention to complete the plan is trustworthy.**
"What I have said, that will I bring about; what I have planned, that will I do" (Isa. 46:11).

• **God controlled the events in Jesus' life. Neither Romans nor Jews could disrupt God's plan.**
"There is no wisdom, no insight, no plan that can succeed against the Lord" (Prov. 21:30).

PUZZLE PIECE
Imagine the Empty Tomb

God's plan came into focus at the death and resurrection of Jesus.
   "In their fright the women bowed down with their faces to the ground, but the men said to them, 'Why do you look for the living among the dead? He is not here; he has risen!'" (Luke 24:5–6).
   Looking at the stick figure of Jesus on the Cross, Taylor and I talked about the friend of Jesus who buried Him. I told Taylor about visiting Jesus' grave in Jerusalem. I said, "The tomb is emp . . ." Before I finished the word *empty,* Taylor interrupted, "I know. God got 'em."

Taylor does not grasp the meaning of God before time. But she has an uncomplicated trust that Jesus was a baby in a bed in a barn; that Jesus' body dripped blood from a cross; that "God got 'em from the grave."

Rejoice with the writer of Lamentations: "The Lord has done what he planned; he has fulfilled his word" (Lam. 2:17).

PART AND PARCEL
A Plan for Each One

Zacchaeus, the guests, and curious spectators who filled Zacchaeus's courtyard were the first to hear Jesus announce God's plan: "For the Son of Man came to seek and to save what was lost" (Luke 19:10). Through faithful witnesses, the plan traveled from Jericho to Melissa Bowen's hometown. She understood that Jesus came to seek and to save her. Hear her story:

"God, because He loves me so, made a plan to bring me to Him and make my life complete. He freed me from sin. His plan was that He sent His Son, Jesus, for me. When I understood this, such joy entered my heart! I could hardly believe it! I accepted the gift that God was holding out to me at that moment, even though I knew I did not deserve it. He brought peace to my heart that night. Many things have happened in my life since that night, some wonderful and some very sad. But the joy and peace I felt so many years ago have always been with me to help celebrate the good things and make them even better, and to help me bear the sad things. God is always with me."

Melissa shares her testimony in her career, in her lifestyle, and on short-term missions trips. "God is always with me" is evident in her cluster of life's pieces.

PUZZLE PIECE
Imagine Tongues of Fire and Wind

Jesus sought out and offered salvation to sinners while He lived on earth. He continues to seek and save the lost through His Holy Spirit Who is present in every believer. In fact, the Holy Spirit accomplishes our part in God's plan.

When Jesus said to His disciples, "I send the promise of my Father upon you" (Luke 24:49 KJV), He knew the sending would be costly. Christ must be crucified, resurrected, and ascend into heaven before the promise could come.

Old Testament prophets stated God's promise in various ways: "Afterward, I will pour out my Spirit on all people" (Joel 2:28); "I will put my Spirit in you" (Ezek. 36:27).

Centuries passed. For all practical purposes, the prophecies had been forgotten. During the closing days of Jesus' ministry, He reminded the disciples of the promise to send the Spirit. He tried to prepare them for His departure. Even so, they were fearful and disheartened. They had depended on Him:

Lord, we will be alone. "I will ask the Father, and He will give you another Helper" (John 14:16 NASB).

Lord, we are ignorant. "The Helper . . . will teach you all things" (John 14:26 NASB).

Lord, we are helpless. "He is the Spirit. . . . He remains with you and is in you" (John 14:17 TEV).

Lord, we will fail in our witness to a hostile world. "When the Holy Spirit comes upon you, you will be filled with power, and you will be witnesses" (Acts 1:8 TEV).

After the Ascension, the perplexed disciples obeyed Jesus' command to wait in Jerusalem for the promised gift.

The promise came spectacularly. A rushing wind dramatized the outpouring of the Holy Spirit. The Spirit, real though unseen, energized and empowered the disciples for service.

Accompanying the wind, a single tongue of fire settled on each person. Fire indicated that God acknowledged the believers as the body of Christ. Fire also represented the fervor to proclaim the gospel. Fire was connected to the tabernacle and temple worship where fire consumed the sacrifice indicating God's acceptance. Now the believers, united and individually, were the new temple—the body of Christ, the church.

The Promise came to unbelievers in the sense that His work was to convince the world of sin (Acts 2:37–42).

The Promise came to the world (Acts 1:8). "God so loved the world" was on Jesus' mind before His ascension. His commission overwhelmed the disciples. Jesus knew God was not regional, nor the gospel isolated in a particular place. Since the plan was not a human instigation, believers could not use their own ingenuity to spread the gospel. The Promise would consecrate the church for its task to evangelize the world. The Spirit, going everywhere within the believers, would translate the gospel into every language and culture. Jesus connected His Spirit with power to serve, not with sanctification.

The Promise came to you and me (Acts 2:39). At the time of conversion, Jesus gives us the Holy Spirit. The onetime experience adds us to the body of Christ.

In the Old Testament, God was for His people. In the Gospels, God was with His people in the person of Jesus. Since Pentecost, God has been in His people. We never need to plead as David, "Do not . . . take your Holy Spirit from me." God never withdraws His presence. We can grieve Him, quench Him, and reject His guidance. He still loves us.

MY PART
My Cluster Has a Witnessing Piece

Tom explained his attempt to reach God through a mixture of beliefs, an incorporation of doctrines from all world religions.

"Tom," I said, "I have good news for you. Let me tell you God's simple plan to reach you."

After listening to the Word describing Jesus' birth, death, and resurrection, Tom responded, "That plan is too simple. There's not enough struggle."

Tom is lost.

Apathy or lack of conviction in lost people limits, even prevents, my part in God's plan. As the criminal was led to the scaffold, the chaplain shared of Christ's power to save. The criminal shouted, "Do you believe it? If I believed it, I would crawl across the continent on broken glass to tell people it is true."

How vital is my belief that lost people need the Lord? The thought for the week in a church bulletin was "Christian, keep the faith . . . but not from others!"

Abraham entrusted Eliezer with the task of winning a bride for Isaac (Gen. 24). Eliezer's plan parallels a worthy plan for us to use in witnessing. Eliezer received his instruction, followed the angel, prayed for success, asked for a sign as to whom to approach, thanked God for answered prayer, delivered the message, encountered opposition, and expected success.

"This is from the Lord," was the response of Rebekah's relatives to Eliezer's efforts (Gen. 24:50).

Many miles separate Tom and me. My continuing prayer is that a Christian will cross his path and discern, "This encounter is from the Lord."

2

GOD'S PLAN *To Reach Out to the Lost*

MY PART *To Reach Up in Faith*

"For all have sinned and fall short of the glory of God, and are justified freely by his grace through the redemption that came by Christ Jesus. God presented him as a sacrifice of atonement, through faith in his blood" (Rom. 3:23–25).

How many pieces are in this puzzle? That was the first question as we stared at the "Tempting Sweets" pile of pieces. Throughout the assemblage, questions were frequent: Has anyone seen a shape that will fit here? Is this piece part of a brownie or a cupcake? Does this corner on a platter go with the malt balls or fudge candy? Would anyone guess how many chocolate chips are in this puzzle? And on and on.

Not all questions are raised as a matter of doubt, objection, or debate. Questions are also inquiries to receive information. In your conversations with God, do you ever ask what, when, where, why, or how? A questioning mind jolts comfortable thoughts and sends us searching deeper into the Scriptures—not entirely for answers but for a closer communion with God.

14

PUZZLE PIECE
Imagine Saul Persecuting Followers of Jesus

Bloodthirsty accurately described Saul's attitude as he stepped onto the Damascus Road (Acts 26:9–11). With the chief priest's permission and under the guise of rescuing Judaism from heretics, Saul led a popular movement to eliminate followers of Jesus. He believed that Jesus blasphemed God by claiming to be God's Son. Saul's motives were linked with brutality.

Bloodbaths in the name of religion are shameful, wicked actions continuing to occur in the twenty-first century. Through the media, scenes of people groups eradicating one another in the name of religion arouse anguish in our hearts and repulsion to our senses.

Do your thoughts ever scream, "What are you people thinking about?"

Ask the questions of Saul. "Saul, what were you thinking about in your attempts to purge society of Jesus' followers?"

"Blood," Saul replies. "My heritage through the bloodline of Benjamin's tribe was taught in our home. My ancestral religion taught that God required blood sacrifices to atone for sin. I believe blood trickled down from Mount Moriah where Abram was willing to slit Isaac's throat on a sacrificial altar (Gen. 22); . . . to Egypt where Hebrew slaves swathed their doorposts with the blood of slaughtered sheep (Ex. 12:13); . . . into the temple where the High Priest entered God's presence and communed with Him only by sprinkling blood around the altar (Ex. 29:16)."

A beneficial devotional exercise is to read the first five books of the Old Testament from the Pharisee Saul's point of view. The study aids in understanding Saul's mind-set and purpose when Luke introduces him at Stephen's stoning: "Meanwhile, the witnesses laid their clothes at the feet of a young man named Saul" (Acts 7:58); and "Saul was there, giving approval to his death" (Acts 8:1).

The New Testament experiences of Saul, and later when he was known as Paul, reveal his personality traits. Two of them were flamboyance and commitment to a cause. I read Leviticus through his eyes. I imagined that Aaron's elaborate ordination (Lev. 8) impressed the young Saul: "Moses slaughtered the ram and took some of its blood and put it on the lobe of Aaron's right ear, on the thumb of his right hand and on the big toe of his right foot" (Lev. 8:23).

The daubing of blood on the ear symbolized welcoming every word from the Lord; on the hand, performing righteous acts; on the foot, walking in the way of God's commandments. The ritual represented cleansing the entire body and consecrating all of a person's energies to God's service.

The symbolism of the ritual would appeal to Saul's flamboyant commitment or excessive pledge to keep Judaism pure. With blood on his ear, Saul's knowledge of the Law motivated him to ensure that the covenant between God and His chosen people remain intact. To Saul, Jews who followed Jesus tampered with the Law— tantamount to denying God. Because of his status and education, Saul loathed the claims of ignorant preachers that a Galilean peasant Who had been crucified had risen from the dead and was the promised Messiah. His nature revolted in disgust that faith in Jesus of Nazareth offered eternal life.

With blood on his hands, Saul persecuted the followers of Jesus. "I put many of the saints in prison, and when they were put to death, I cast my vote against them" (Acts 26:10).

With blood on his feet, Saul tracked down followers of Jesus. He systematically began to destroy the church. "Going from house to house, he dragged off men and women and put them in prison" (Acts 8:3).

Saul called his rampage against believers an obsession (Acts 26:11). His devotion to God convinced him that his purge of Jesus' followers honored God. Saul's studious nature and keen mind misunderstood God's plan. He became God's chief persecutor.

Saul's thirst for blood would not be quenched while any believer in Jesus lived. "Breathing out murderous threats against the Lord's disciples" (Acts 9:1), Saul approached Damascus as an aggressive, influential enemy.

On the 150-mile hike from Jerusalem to Damascus, Saul had hours to consider events in the life of Jesus of Nazareth. The fact that Jesus applied a popular secular proverb to Saul's state of mind suggests that Jesus knew the struggles within Saul. The proverb "It is hard for you to kick against the goads" (Acts 26:14) described a method of training unbroken oxen. Punching the animal with a sharp stick hurt the oxen. The animal finally learned that submitting to the path chosen by the owner was the best way.

Perhaps Saul's conscience struggled with:
- Stephen's demeanor as he died like a saint not a criminal.
- Stephen's blood because later Paul wrote he knew that moral consent carried as much responsibility as throwing the stones (Rom. 1:32).
- his own fascination at Stephen's vision of seeing Jesus standing at God's right hand.
- the followers of Jesus thriving on persecution. J. Winston Pearce described the movement like a fire beginning small "in Jerusalem. . . . It rages throughout Judea; it has leaped into Samaria; it burns in Galilee; its flames are seen in distant Damascus."

- the Law pointing to a way of satisfaction; yet not satisfying his needs. The very commandment that promised life, he wrote, "actually brought death" (Rom. 7:10).
- his cruel intolerance. Hints of Saul's doubts appear in his letters. For example, "It is fine to be zealous, provided the purpose is good" (Gal. 4:18).

    Perhaps Saul questioned:
- What if my righteousness is not enough?
- What if Stephen saw the Son of man standing at the right hand of God? (Acts 7:56)
- What if Stephen was correct that the Righteous One was betrayed and murdered? (Acts 7:52)
- What if Jesus of Nazareth was alive? If God raised Jesus from the dead, God declared Him to be the Son of God. God would never raise up a blasphemer.

Saul tried to stifle the pricks of his conscience. By stating the proverb, Jesus reminded Saul that he was hurting himself; that to resist a superior power was useless. No doubt, Jesus put a notion in Saul's mind that later the writer of Hebrews expanded into these words: "How much more, then, will the blood of Christ, who through the eternal spirit offered himself unblemished to God, cleanse our consciences from acts that lead to death, so that we may serve the living God!" (Heb. 9:14). A pricked conscience was not enough to stop Saul's rampage.

PUZZLE PIECE
Imagine Saul Kneeling on the Damascus Road

One day about noon, Saul and his entourage arrogantly marched toward Damascus. Suddenly "a light from heaven, brighter than the sun," blazed around them (Acts 26:13). Losing his balance, Saul fell to the ground. Simultaneously his former life collapsed. Saul knew how

God had called the names Moses and Samuel. Now the voice distinctly called, "Saul."

Jesus' first words, "Saul, why do you persecute me?" penetrated Saul's soul. Saul loved God. His intention was to defend, not persecute, God. Jesus' question contained an overwhelming revelation. Saul realized that by persecuting Jesus' followers, he had again and again harmed God Whom he adored.

Jesus' question challenged Saul to give a reason for his excessive zeal against believers of the Way. At another time Saul could have eloquently justified his theology. Now he only wanted to know the name of the speaker. Jesus responded with His human name that Saul hated. "I am Jesus of Nazareth" (Acts 22:8). Confronted by his enemy, Saul, whose usual flow of words had such force, stammered, "What shall I do, Lord?" (Acts 22:10).

Think of Saul's question from different points of view.

"What shall I do, Lord, for You?" With an emphasis on *I*, Saul's natural trait as a doer surfaced. God did have a plan for Saul to do. At the emotionally charged moment kneeling under God's searchlight was not the time or place to learn his destiny.

"What shall I do, Lord, for salvation?" Nothing! "For it is by grace you have been saved, through faith—and this not from yourselves, it is the gift of God" (Eph 2:8). On the way to Damascus, Saul experienced what he later preached, "For all have sinned and fall short of the glory of God, and are justified freely by his grace through the redemption that came by Christ Jesus. God presented him as a sacrifice of atonement, through faith in his blood" (Rom. 3:23–25). Saul was on a mission to shed blood because of grace. Paul learned a truth we too have experienced: Grace is God's part in reaching out to us. Faith is my part in reaching up to God.

The blood trickling down from Mount Moriah, to Egypt, through sacrificial offerings, into the temple finally flowed through Jesus on the Cross. Saul, kneeling beneath it, felt the drops until his spirit was absorbed into the life of Christ. "I no longer live, but Christ lives in me" (Gal. 2:20).

"What shall I do, Lord, for You?" Obey! Maybe in an instant before his blindness, Saul saw the same imploring look of Jesus that Peter had seen. Later Paul wrote to the Corinthians about "the light of the knowledge of the glory of God in the face of Christ" (2 Cor. 4:6).

Yielding to the power and authority of Christ tempered Saul's question. He surrendered his stern will and obeyed the Lord's instruction, "Get up . . . and go into Damascus" (Acts 22:10). From that moment Saul was committed to God's plan, whatever it might be.

MY PART
My Cluster Has a Salvation Piece

Have you ever thought, "I wish I had had a Damascus Road experience like Paul"? You did have the experience, only not identical to Paul's.

In Sue Tatum's younger years when someone spoke emotionally of a dramatic conversion experience, she would question momentarily her own calm, deliberate, minimally emotional—but real—encounter with the Savior. Sue reminds us, "I've often felt we magnify and overemphasize dramatic experiences without making it abundantly clear that circumstances surrounding salvation experiences differ from person to person."

Ann Street Hill where I accepted Jesus as Savior was a world away from the road leading to Damascus, but the same light shined into my soul.

All the children in our neighborhood liked to compete in bicycle races up and down Ann Street Hill. Staying vertical was a challenge. To conquer the steep hill, I had to gather speed two blocks away. The momentum, aided by strenuous puffing and pumping, propelled the bike over the hill.

Ann Street was also the route I rode my bike to Vacation Bible School. Every day Mrs. Rooks impressed our class of nine-year-olds with the meaning of John 3:16. Every day the hill loomed higher. Somber thoughts about sin and my need for a Savior weighed on my heart and sapped my physical strength. Then one noon as Ann Street Hill came into view, I asked Jesus to be my Savior. In an instant, I was over the top happy, unburdened, free!

What happened at the foot of Ann Street Hill? A child was born again. I trusted God in the same way Paul did. He described our salvation experience like this: "For it is by grace you have been saved, through faith—and this not from yourselves, it is the gift of God—not by works, so that no one can boast" (Eph. 2:8–9).

My! What an extravagant gift: undeserved forgiveness for all my sins and a right standing with God; a binding love relationship that nothing can sever; release from the law and freedom to grow under grace into the likeness of Christ; my own personal place in the body of Christ, the church; the presence of Christ's Spirit within me; eternal life. Each of these mercies to which my childlike yes responded is equally significant.

At the foot of Ann Street Hill, I found grace, not condemnation or vengeance; but the unearned, undeserved, incredible kindness of God. The first step of my part in God's plan was to receive forgiveness of my sins.

Paul had a Damascus Road experience that he readily shared. I have an Ann Street Hill experience to talk about. You have a momentous salvation moment to tell about.

In regard to witnessing, the Holy Spirit needs three things from us:

1. The memory of our salvation experience. The maturing process moves us away from the enthusiasm of the initial encounter with Jesus. Regularly relishing the time when God entrusted us with a part of Himself—His Son—keeps the experience fresh.

2. Our knowledge of certain Scriptures that the Holy Spirit will use to convince and convict others of sin. Our comments about God's Word do not save. The Word made flesh does.

3. Our availability. Our prayers are not, "Lord, give me an opportunity to witness"; but, "Lord, discipline me to take advantage of the opportunities I have." Being available to tell my story based on Scripture is my part in God's plan.

PART AND PARCEL
Sue's Witness to Alice

Sue teaches Bible studies in a nursing home. She was concerned about one particular resident. Alice was "crusty," sometimes antagonistic, and spiritually lost. People had witnessed to her over her lifetime of 90 years. Her health was in rapid decline and one leg had been removed.

One Sunday, Sue was drawn to Alice's bedside when she seemed unusually alert. Sue recalls, "Without design on my part, I began talking loudly into her ear about Jesus. I realized Alice was really hearing me. 'Alice, don't you think it's time for you to let Jesus save you?'"

Her immediate reply was, "Yes, I'd like to do that." Alice prayed to receive Jesus as her Savior and we all shed some tears. Isn't the Holy Spirit a better programmer than we are?"

PUZZLE PIECE
Imagine Jesus' Baptism

Jesus promised to keep His part in God's plan. Commitment is crucial to accomplish God's plan. In fact, God presided over Jesus' unique surrender of Himself to the will of the Father. The Holy Spirit, descending in the form of a dove, was reminiscent of the Spirit hovering, fluttering in the divine activity of creation. The Holy Spirit empowered Jesus for His public ministry. Accompanying the dove was a verbal acceptance from His Father revealing that He was the Chosen One of God and that the Cross was His destiny (Psalm 2:7; Isa. 42:11).

The commitment was reciprocal. Jesus surrendered completely to God, and God entrusted Jesus with the redemption of lost people. Jesus' commitment was not just a happy occasion to cherish. It thrust Him into the mainstream of life in Palestine. Jesus' commitment was demonstrated through personal encounters with people in His routine.

MY PART
My Cluster Has a Commitment Piece

Do you ever feel that you allow secular interests to dominate your lifestyle?

Do you promote self rather than the treasure that self contains?

The surrendered life places priority on God's plan.

The surrendered life makes decisions and choices on the answer to the question, What would Jesus do?

The surrendered life could be anonymous ministries privately celebrating the treasure within.

The surrendered life thrusts us into the mainstream

of the community. In the arena of relationships, we become channels of God's blessings.

Can you identify with my chagrin at this encounter? As my son and I shopped, the cashier noticed our jovial mood. She mentioned, "You and you son are having a good time." With a heavy sigh, she continued, "My life is such a drag."

Driving home, I asked, "Barton, did you hear the cashier's remark about life being a drag?"

"Yessum."

"I'm sorry that I used our rush as an excuse to walk away. I should have stopped to tell her about my joy in Jesus Christ."

Instead, I missed the moment Christ prepared for me to share His splendor. I can never recall that moment of readiness.

Perhaps you have missed a moment in sharing your faith. Instead of fearing inadequacy for future witnessing encounters, let us allow the mistakes to motivate us to be more attentive to the Spirit's nudges and more respon-sive to our part in God's plan.

When I allow the Holy Spirit to minister and witness through me, I never think about the actual time or place of commitment. When I deny Him the use of my life, the memory of the commitment convicts me that I have reduced the Lord's glory to a dim glow. He throbs for an outlet.

3

GOD'S PLAN   *To Offer Grace*
MY PART   *To Receive Grace*

"But by the grace of God I am what I am" (1 Cor. 15:10).

Late in the evening when the family members had retired, I returned to the puzzle. Lamplight bathed the pieces in a soft glow. My intention was to sit still and enjoy the progress of the incomplete puzzle, "Tempting Sweets." Although the activity of the day had subsided, my thoughts echoed lively conversations sprinkled with laughter and the jockeying for positions around the table. I relished the quiet reflection of how connecting pieces of a puzzle contributed to family unity.

The hubbub of daily life can hush the silences when we most clearly hear God's voice. Tranquil moments enable us to feel emotions within the soul. Emotions like gratitude for grace nourish our desire to be and to do our part in God's plan.

Grace is the foundation of God's plan. Grace is love in action: "For it is by grace you have been saved, through faith—and this not from yourselves, it is the gift of God" (Eph. 2:8).

One of seven children, the little boy was hospitalized because of an accident. His family was very poor. Their hunger was never satisfied. Two children always shared a full glass of milk. In the hospital, a nurse handed the child a large glass of cold milk. He eagerly reached out and then drew back his hand as he remembered sharing with the other children. "How deep can I drink?" he asked.

With a lump in her throat, the nurse replied, "Drink all of it. Drink all of it."

How deep can we drink from the love and goodness of God? No limit! We can drink it again and again. God's grace is inexhaustible.

PUZZLE PIECE
Imagine an Acrostic of God's Grace

Gifted
Redeemed
Awakened
Called
Empowered

The acrostic defines five elements of God's grace. Allow the ideas to refresh your spirit in the richness (Eph. 1:7; 2:7) and the abundance (Rom. 5:17,20) of grace.

G ifted. The Holy Spirit assigned us one or more spiritual gifts the day we were born again. Always pointing to Jesus, the Holy Spirit gives us gifts enabling us to honor and serve the Lord. The gifts build up the Lord's body, the Church. He plans for us to use our gifts within a sphere of service. Recognizing your spiritual gift(s) helps you know your part in God's plan. Just as puzzle pieces are unequal in size and color, gifts are individualized.

Women who confirm their gifts have a happy sense of freedom in knowing they are special. Confirming your gift eliminates low self-esteem. An unhealthy self-image with the accompanying feelings of inadequacy and inferiority is a heavy burden to carry through life. Good news! God has graced your unique personality with a unique gift. You are able to minister through your gift in ways not duplicated in any other person. You are competent!

God has appointed you a particular place in His body, the Church. Since the Holy Spirit empowers the gift, you will accomplish the purpose that God has in mind for you. Knowing your gift is mercy, teaching, or helping, you do not consider yourself worthless or competitive because you are not an evangelist, an exhorter, or an administrator. You belong!

God has promised you will never lose your usefulness, "For the gifts and calling of God are without repentance" (Rom. 11:29 KJV). You are secure.

Your gift points you to your part in God's plan.

Saying, "Thank You, Lord, for saving me" is a daily, sincere expression of gratitude through prayer. Showing gratitude by ministering through my gift is an enthusiastic way to celebrate the occasion of my rebirth.

R edeemed. When the Hebrews desired to remember a person or a place, they traced the object of affection on their palms. By puncturing the outline with a sharp instrument and rubbing dye into the holes, an indelible imprint remained in the palm. "I have inscribed you on the palms of My hands" (Isa. 49:16 NASB).

Your name carved with spikes and spelled with blood in Jesus' hands is covenant love. In your imagination, reach for the Lord's palm. Gaze at your name. Trace it in His blood and remember His sacrifice. The only credential we have for being a part of His plan is that our names are carved in the Lord's palm.

Because you see your name, thank God for covenant love that cannot be canceled or withdrawn. Thank Him that no calamity can remove you from His thoughts and care. Thank the Father for covenant love that revives, renews, and disciplines. Thank God for covenant love that allows you to suffer patiently as He leads you down roads you did not anticipate. Thank God for covenant love that keeps you on His mind and always in His heart.

A wakened. Imagine that you accompanied Jesus as He walked among the churches in your community: Crossroads, First, Suburbia. But He never ventured through the doors. With piercing vision, He discerned the true name of each church—Sardis! Sardis, flattered with its reputation in the community of being alive, was really dead. Dead orthodoxy, dead correctness caused the church to drift into the peril of replacing God's grace with a frenzy of activity.

Jesus knew the truth. Sardis had ceased to matter. Those seeking spiritual sustenance found nothing at Sardis. In this decaying congregation, a faithful few kept Sardis from being an animated corpse.

God issued a wake-up call: "Wake up! Strengthen what remains and is about to die. . . . Remember, therefore, what you have received and heard; obey it, and repent" (Rev. 3:2–3). If Jesus addressed the wake-up call to you, would He need a fire alarm or a gentle hum?

C alled. Being called is a summons to a lifestyle of grace. All people are called to repentance, forgiveness, salvation; to love, fellowship, obedience; to consecration, dedication, and stewardship.

We are called children of God—heirs.

We are called different—holy.

We are called disciples—doers of God's plan.

We are called light. Jesus said, "I am the light of the world" (John 8:12). He gave us His image when He said, "You are . . . light."

We are called letters. God's message is written on our hearts (2 Cor. 3:3).

God's call is a divine command to people. In Isaiah 45:3, God called the Hebrews to be His chosen people: "I am the Lord, the God of Israel, who summons you by name." Writing to the Philippians, Paul spoke about a heavenward call.

At times God called individuals to particular roles. God called Amos, Ezekiel, Hosea, Isaiah, Jeremiah, and Samuel to prophesy.

God called Saul and David to become Israel's kings.

Peter, Andrew, James, and John answered Jesus' call to join His ministry.

God called Paul to be a missionary to the Gentiles.

God called Matthew and Cheryl Nance to South Korea. Their testimony highlights their call.

"We came to Korea in 1990. During the past years, we have experienced unexpected challenges, including loneliness, isolation, rats chewing through our plastic food containers, deaths and births of family members without us there, sudden surgeries, cross-cultural conflict, strains in relating to other missionaries, and stomachaches from eating too much dried squid. What is the one thing that has given us the power to stay?

"There is only one answer in every case. The call of God fills His people with a consuming passion that the lost come to know and worship Him.

"Do not think that the call of God to missionary service results primarily in suffering in the life of the missionary. The call of God results primarily in great joy, satisfaction, and a deep sense of purpose in life."

God's call is synonymous to His enablings. What He calls us to do, He is prepared to accomplish.

PART AND PARCEL
Girls in Action Respond to a Temporary Need

After learning about carnival chaplains, the girls asked, "Who's the chaplain that comes with the carnival to our county fair?"

"Small carnivals do not have chaplains," I replied. With that comment, the girls erupted in excitement, "We could be! Could we be? Oh, let's be!"

My eyes met Sherry's, the coleader, and we knew the meaning of called. We knew when the carnival pulled into town, 13 young chaplains would meet it.

The girls decided to serve a meal and to distribute tracts. With permission from the fair officials, we made arrangements with the manager of the carnival. On the designated day, men from the church set up long tables in the clean hog barn. The women filled the tables with stick-to-your-ribs food. The girls stacked and restacked tracts and New Testaments they had studied in order to share.

At the appointed time, we welcomed the tired, dusty, oily men into the barn. They had worked almost two days assembling the carnival rides and exhibits. They gazed at the food like it was manna from heaven. One said, "We eat mostly bologna."

After prayer, our guests filled their plates. At this point, the girls, hidden behind Sherry and me, whispered, "We are scared. We don't want to talk to them."

Sherry wisely said, "Pray for courage. When the men are seated, if you feel like you want to speak to one, do it. But if you do not feel like you should speak, remember helping at the tables is ministry too."

Finally all were seated and eating. Christy said, "I'll take a tract to him," pointing to a young blond man. We watched as Christy approached him, began a conversation, and opened the tract. Encouraged that the first encounter went well, the other girls grabbed tracts and New Testaments. For the next 30 minutes that hog barn was a beehive of activity and sweet sharing. One of the girls, rushing past me, breathlessly asked, "Miss Stuart, who are the missionaries, them or us?"

In a missions meeting, 13 little girls opened a magazine. They learned about carnival chaplains. They connected their new knowledge to a need in our town. They followed through in ministry and witness. Called? Yes!

The girls, Sherry, and I learned that when we are in the middle of God's activity, we most clearly understand our part in His plan.

E mpowered. Thank You, Father, for powerful grace working in us and causing us to admit our nothingness apart from You. Thank You for powerful grace giving us endurance to live Jesus' principles in a carnal society.

Thank You, Father, for explosive grace—the excitement of being filled with Your priorities.

Thank You, Father, for blazing grace that whispers, shouts, and cries out my name; that gives inner strength enabling outward gentleness and sensitivity to feel another's pain.

Thank You for blazing grace that fuels my faith.

Thank You, Father, for pulsating grace that releases Your energy through us. We acknowledge that every victory and accomplishment comes from Your Spirit.

We feel the throb of Your powerful grace, Your explosive grace, Your blazing grace, and Your pulsating grace.

Humbly we grasp the reality that Your grace is in "jars of clay to show that this all-surpassing power is from God and not from us" (2 Cor. 4:7). Amen.

MY PART
My Cluster Has an Acrostic of Grace

Gifted. Consider specific ways your grace gifts encourage your competence, your sense of belonging, and your self-worth.

Redeemed. In what ways have you felt the security of God's covenant love?

Awakened. Decide to learn something fresh about God's grace as we make Isaiah's wake-up call our own: "He wakens me morning by morning, wakens my ear to listen like one being taught" (Isa. 50:4).

Called. I asked friends, "How do you stay sensitive in your call?" All replied through Bible study and prayer. In addition, Virginia Cartwright mentioned fellowship with friends and a constant awareness of peoples' hurts.

The Sunday morning worship service challenges Camilla Lowry to stay sensitive. She explains, "It satisfies, yet intensifies, my hunger to come back to God and to do His will."

Empowered. How does God's grace empower and equip you to do your part in God's plan?

The word *grace* is like a burst of sunlight. Perhaps I associate grace with light because of Paul's encounter with the Lord, the "true light that shines on everyone" (John 1:9 CEV). God's plan is for us to fulfill the prophecy of Isaiah 49:6: "For this is what the Lord has commanded us: 'I have made you a light for the Gentiles, that you may bring salvation to the ends of the earth'" (Acts 13:47).

4

GOD'S PLAN *To Call and Prepare*
MY PART *To Respond and Yield*

"But when God, who set me apart from birth and called me by his grace, was pleased to reveal his Son in me so that I might preach him among the Gentiles" (Gal. 1:15).

Working on the "Tempting Sweets" puzzle, often we randomly placed pieces with no intention of finishing the nuts on a brownie or the icing on a cupcake. Of course, the pieces were necessary for the puzzle's completion; but at the moment of placement they seemed like pieces without a purpose.

In God's plan, some conditions or situations with respect to our personalities, places, or people seem incidental or even nonessential—like pieces without a purpose. In retrospect, we see how God did not waste any instant. All of life's experiences prepare us to do our part in God's plan to seek and to save the lost.

On the stretch of road into Damascus, Saul could not see God's total plan for his life. He did not take a giant step from Damascus to Rome. God did not zap Saul with instant insight about how to become the great missionary Paul. God does not prepare a life and then decide its purpose. Life is not put on hold during preparation. The process of becoming the part God intends lies in the minutiae of day-to-day living. Every experience, important in itself, prepares us for the next experience. Many steps readied Saul for a missionary career. God, our Father, is a faithful nurturer.

God called Saul to a ministry among the Gentiles. However, his concern for the Jews never diminished. He loved the Jews to the extent that he would have given up his own hope of eternity if he could have saved them (Rom. 9:3; 10:1).

Saul of Tarsus met God's criteria for the missionary He needed to both Jews and Gentiles. The preparation for Saul's ministry began from his birth. God chose Saul from a particular background with specific credentials that would benefit the ministry and even save Saul's life.

PUZZLE PIECE
Imagine a Road Sign: Tarsus of Cilicia, Roman Colony

God planned for Saul's birth in a Roman city (Acts 22:28). With a population of a half million, Tarsus was an ancient city when Saul was born. In a 38 B.C. historical incident, Cleopatra sailed her luxurious rowboat down the Cydnus River into the middle of Tarsus to meet Mark Antony. With a harbor on the Mediterranean Sea in addition to the Cydnus River, Tarsus was an accessible commercial and military center. Two major highways intersected in Tarsus, making travel convenient. Tourists regularly attended cultural events, athletic contests, and pagan religious rites there.

Mark Antony made Tarsus an autonomous city with the privileges of self-government, duty-free import and export trade, and the production of their own coins. Artisans inscribed *Loveliest, Greatest Metropolis* on the coins. As Jews who inherited Roman citizenship, Saul's family was among the city's aristocracy.

Cloth made from goat hair was the major industry in Tarsus. The goats, grazing on the foothills of the Taurus mountains, were valued for their magnificent silky hair. The woven fabrics and tanned skins were in demand throughout the Roman Empire. Since all boys were apprenticed to a business, Saul learned to weave tent cloth and to prepare animal hides for tents at the goat-hair cloth establishment.

Descriptions and analogies in Paul's letters indicate the city's influence on the young Saul. Later, Paul's civic patriotism and sense of citizenship responsibility were evident in his response to soldiers in Jerusalem who questioned his identity. Paul said, "I am a Jew, from Tarsus in Cilicia, a citizen of no ordinary city" (Acts 22:25–39).

In his teaching, Paul applied the importance of citizenship to Christians' allegiance to God and to one another: "You are no longer foreigners and aliens, but fellow citizens with God's people and members of God's household" (Eph. 2:19; see also Phil. 3:20 and Eph. 2:12). Paul encouraged Christians to fulfill civic duties as a way to reflect God's love.

Living in Tarsus gave Paul sympathy for city life. He was not intimidated by the lifestyle of the multitudes of people in Corinth, Ephesus, and Rome. In Tarsus, Paul attended the public games. He used athletic illustrations to explain that the Christian life requires discipline and preparation (1 Cor. 9:24).

PUZZLE PIECE
Imagine the Ten Commandments on Stone Tablets

God planned for Saul's birth into a devout Hebrew family. His heritage was through the bloodline of

Benjamin's tribe, which had a unique place in history. Benjamin was the only patriarch who had been born in the Promised Land. When Israel went into battle, Benjamin's tribe held the place of honor. The battle cry was "After thee, O Benjamin." The name Saul honored his ancestor, King Saul. The name Paul indicated his Roman citizenship. When Saul became a missionary to the Gentiles, he used his Roman name.

Saul's father was a Pharisee who strictly observed and taught the Hebrew laws and customs (Phil. 3:4–8). No doubt, the family rejected the pagan practices of the majority of the citizens in Tarsus. According to Jewish custom, Saul's merchant father would never buy items from heathen businessmen for three days before pagan festivals. They might spend the money to buy idols or give an offering to their pagan gods. Jewish families never visited non-Jewish friends on special occasions because they would make offerings to their gods.

Saul's family lived in a Jewish settlement where the government allowed the Jews to control the religious rites in the synagogue. As a child, Saul learned about the special relationship between God and the Jews. The law was the covenant that bound God to His people. To deny the law was to deny God. In his home and with the rabbis, Saul studied God's plan through the Old Testament prophets, enabling him to converse with Jewish leaders in the future.

God planned to use Saul's venturesome, versatile personality. Paul's autobiographical references in his letters describe a moral, law-abiding, honorable man before his conversion. He had never disgraced God.

God needed Saul's aggressive personality to take the gospel to difficult places. Salvation brought the presence of the Holy Spirit into Saul's life with a hefty dose of discipline to control his intense personality.

Salvation preserved Saul's individuality. He always had been a bold speaker. Salvation did not cause him to knuckle under to human authorities. When the High Priest condemned Paul without a hearing, Paul called him a "whitewashed wall" and "a violator of the law" (Acts 23:3). Acts 16:35–37 recalls another bold encounter.

Salvation did not change Saul beyond recognition. He still had a fighter instinct. But the Holy Spirit directed his pugnacious nature toward a new purpose. He was able to say about his ministry, "I have fought the good fight" (2 Tim. 4:7). Throughout his ministry his only weapon was his story of grace.

Saul possessed a remarkable singleness of purpose. His excessive zeal focused on the destruction of Christians and the eradication of Jesus' name from history. Vacillation was not a part of his nature.

Paul was traditional in his principles, never yielding in debates. On the other hand, his methods were radical. Not stereotyped, he suited the messages to the audience: to Jews in the synagogues and Greek philosophers at the Acropolis; to pagan crowds at Lystra and court assemblies before Roman rulers. Paul explained his method. "To the weak I became weak, to win the weak. I have become all things to all men so that by all possible means I might save some" (1 Cor. 9:22).

PART AND PARCEL
On the Job

Linette Hall lives in Kingston, Jamaica, with her husband, Sydney Hall, pastor of Mamby Park Baptist Church, and their children, Abigail and Stephen.

As a young woman entering the workforce, Linette felt her greatest weakness was her ability to identify error because in the process she seemed to offend many people. Not long after she began working, her aptitude for finding errors caused difficulty. One day, in something she was reading about the life of Paul, the writer highlighted the great zeal with which Saul had persecuted the Christians. He emphasized that Saul's zeal was not necessarily a flaw because after his conversion, he served the Lord with that same zeal. That day Linette committed her critical nature to God. She asked Him to use it positively.

Linette's ability for finding errors is perfect for her job today as editorial assistant for Caribbean Christian Publication's Bible Lessons. She finds mistakes and makes corrections, allowing the editors to focus on other responsibilities. She thanks God that He transformed a great weakness into a great strength.

PUZZLE PIECE
Imagine Saul Reading a Scroll

God planned for Saul to live in an intellectual environment. Tarsus ranked with Alexandria and Athens as an erudite university city. Under famous tutors, Saul learned to speak and read Greek, to debate persuasively, to understand Stoicism—the most influential philosophy at the time. Paul used these skills throughout his ministry. For example, in a mob incident recorded in Acts 21:37–38, Paul's ability to speak Greek impressed the arresting officer. By speaking in Greek, Paul showed he was a cultured, educated man, not a rebel starting riots in the streets. Protected by the officer, Paul gave his defense.

Growing up as a Jew in Tarsus, Saul became savvy in two cultures. He could talk sensibly to Jews and clearly to new Christians in the Roman society. Many of the doctrines and teachings of Jesus, based on the Old Testament, were completely foreign to Gentiles. Paul could express the truth in ways that the pagan mind could grasp.

For example, when citizens in Corinth confessed, "Jesus is Lord," the Holy Spirit gave them spiritual gifts to minister in Corinth. Influenced by the competitiveness of their corrupt culture and their immoral cults, the new believers were confused about how to use their many gifts. Their vitality endangered their worship. Having a fondness for the spectacular, they competed for prominence. Because the new Christians sought individual pre-eminence, their gifts led to rivalry. And so Paul wrote to them, "The Spirit's presence is shown in some way in each person for the good of all" (1 Cor. 12:7 TEV).

Paul borrowed an illustration from their Latin tradition to teach the unity of the varied gifts. Roman historians compared the political state to the human body. The philosopher Plato compared their cities to the human body. For Corinthians, unfamiliar with the Hebrew covenant concept, the body was an appropriate symbol of unity (1 Cor. 12:12–26). A Palestinian Jew, like Peter, would have had difficulty effectively conversing about unity with the Corinthians.

PUZZLE PIECE
Imagine Saul with Gamaliel

In regard to Saul's education, fast-forward his life to Jerusalem and his instruction under Gamaliel. Around the age of 12, Saul moved to Jerusalem where his sister probably lived. The assumption is based on the fact that years later Saul's nephew had access to the barracks in Jerusalem. He warned Saul about the murder plot recorded in Acts 23:16.

The move allowed Saul to become a disciple of Gamaliel (Acts 22:3). The rabbi, respected expert on religious law, gave Saul deep insight into the Old Testament. Because of the emphasis on Gamaliel's knowledge, a major contribution of Gamaliel to Saul is easily overlooked. Historians suggest that Gamaliel "held a . . . spiritual view of the Law, and encouraged Jews to have friendships and social relationships with foreigners."[1] This inclusive advice, an unusual quality of a rabbi, benefited Paul as he ministered in a Gentile world.

God needed a mind like Paul's. Paul presented himself as a high achiever. "I was advancing in Judaism beyond many Jews of my own age and was extremely zealous to the traditions of my fathers" (Gal. 1:14). Paul's speeches and letters recorded in the Scriptures show the thoroughness of his education. He could communicate in Aramaic, Greek, and Latin. He presented accurate knowledge of the Old Testament. His remarkable literary skill has presented God's plan through generations.

PUZZLE PIECE
Imagine a Map Showing a Circuit of Cities

Forcing maturity on a person is often tragic. Preparing Paul for his ministry, God applied a principle about growth. Jesus had expressed to His disciples, "First the stalk, then the head, then the full kernel in the head" (Mark 4:28). Transition from one condition to another is necessary for growth. God planned a strategy to change Paul from persecutor to preacher. After Saul's conversion, God equipped him to preach the gospel and to face difficulties in a restricted, familiar area. Then He launched Paul's career as a missionary to distant cities in the Roman Empire.

Paul's transition began in a sightless condition on Straight Street in Damascus. To await God's time and His plan was an important lesson that God initiated at Judas's house (Acts 9:10–12). From Damascus, the Lord led Paul to Arabia (Gal. 1:15–17). There in seclusion with the Lord, he had time to reflect on his theological convictions and to rethink his understanding of Old Testament teachings.

From Arabia, Paul revisited Damascus where he preached in the synagogue proving that Jesus is the Messiah (Acts 9:22). From Damascus he fled to Jerusalem to escape a Jewish plot to kill him.

In Jerusalem, Paul received the cold shoulder from the disciples. His tarnished reputation caused them to doubt his sincerity. He met Peter and incensed the Jews by his bold preaching. Barnabas, admired by the disciples, defended Paul in spite of the risk.

From Jerusalem to escape another mob, he fled to Caesarea where he boarded a boat to Tarsus. During his protected years in Tarsus, Paul may have planted the churches in the province of Cilicia that are mentioned in Acts 15:41. Surely during the years in Tarsus, Paul was not silent about the Lord he had recently come to know.

In the meantime, while Paul resided in Tarsus, refugees from Jerusalem traveled to Antioch, the Roman administrative capital of the East. Antioch's paved streets were lined with agoras, or shopping malls, where half a million people shopped. Extravagant lighting throughout the city made the night as bright as day.[2]

Citizens and tourists filled the theaters and racing arenas to watch their favorite actors, dancers, and charioteers. They participated in sensual religious rites to their Greek nymph, Daphne. Life in Antioch gave Paul an inkling of the lewdness he would face in Corinth and Ephesus.

The refugee believers evangelized the Gentiles (Acts 11:19–20). The Jerusalem church sent Barnabas to check out the unusual mixture of Jews and Gentiles in the Antioch church. When Barnabas saw "evidence of the grace of God," he knew the perfect preacher for the Antioch believers. Barnabas traveled to Tarsus, enlisted Paul's help, and brought him to Antioch (Acts 11:26).

For a year, "Barnabas and Saul met with the church and taught great numbers of people. The disciples were called Christians first at Antioch" (Acts 11:26). "The Greek word for 'were called' suggests being named after one's business."[3] Nonbelievers watching the lifestyle of believers named them Christians because they were doing the business of Christ.

Antioch was the last preparatory place for Paul's ministry. From there Paul carried the message of Jesus to major cities of the Roman world. Within a relatively small circuit of cities, the Lord walked Paul through a pattern that would be repeated on his missionary journeys: Paul preached boldly in the name of the Lord. He faced opposition in Jewish centers like Jerusalem and in sordid centers of paganism like Antioch. He debated. He took seriously threats of death. He fled. He began again.

Remember in Damascus when the Lord instructed Ananias to minister to the blind Saul? The Lord explained, "I will show him how much he must suffer for my name" (Acts 9:16).

As we live through events, they appear permanent; but as we move away from them, we realize all that happened to us was preparation for the future.

PUZZLE PIECE
Imagine Friends Surrounding Paul

God planned to care for Paul through the ministry of

people. On the Damascus road, Jesus could have out-
lined Paul's life from his conversion to his martyrdom.
Instead Jesus enlisted helpers. He instructed Saul, "Now
get up and go into the city, and you will be told what you
must do" (Acts 9:6).

Incidents recorded in letters to the churches reveal
Paul as a gregarious man with the capacity to sincerely
love people even in his impatience with them. He possessed the ability to hold the loyalty of his friends. He was
gracious in his compliments. When separated from
friends, he expressed loneliness. The Lord knew that
Paul would respond to advice and encouragement from
people.

Ananias influenced Paul in the beginning of his ministry. Ananias, a believer in Damascus, was sensitive to the
Lord's communication through a vision. He was a devout
man with a good reputation. Ananias had the unenviable
responsibility to visit the man whose murderous mission
was well known. Although not enthusiastic about the
assignment, he obeyed the Lord's instruction. Perhaps
the Lord's reminder that Saul was praying and waiting
for Him softened the request and relieved some fear.

Blind, alone, in deep thought, Saul probably was star-
tled by Ananias's touch. Have you ever waited on the
Lord wondering why? Wishing to know the answers?
Speculating about the future? And then with sudden
accuracy the pieces fell into place?

This is what happened to Saul. A stranger entered the
room. He welcomed Saul as a brother demonstrating
Christ's grace and one person's acceptance of another.

His touch restored Saul's sight. He identified Saul's
part in God's plan: "The God that our ancestors worshiped has chosen you to know what he wants done. He
has chosen you to see the One Who obeys God and to
hear his voice" (Acts 22:14–15 CEV).

God used an obscure man to introduce a mighty missionary to his career.

Consider Barnabas's contribution to Paul's part in God's plan. Barnabas, Son of Encouragement, was the nickname given to Joseph, a Levite from Cyprus, by the apostles (Acts 4:36). Evidently Barnabas had instilled hope and confidence in the Jerusalem church. He supported the ministry with his possessions and exhorted the fainthearted with his kind personality. His reputation as "good man, full of the Holy Spirit and faith" was evident in his relationships.

Barnabas was probably a handsome man. When Paul had healed the sick in Lystra, the citizens thought he and Barnabas were gods. They called Barnabas, Zeus. Statues of Zeus present him as a robust, handsome figure (Acts 14:11–12).

When the disciples rebuffed Paul's attempts to join them in Jerusalem, Barnabas interceded and convinced them of their former enemy's conversion. Barnabas had a vision for expanding the Christian church. He, along with Paul, accepted the Antioch church's commission to begin the first organized missionary activity. Through the years, Barnabas quietly influenced the more aggressive Paul. Even their disagreement did not destroy Paul's respect. He always spoke of Barnabas with appreciation.

In the meantime, as Paul pursued his part in God's plan, God prepared a variety of helpful people to intersect his path.

• Silas, a Roman citizen, was a leader in the Jerusalem church. He helped soothe harsh feelings in the Jewish-Gentile problems. As Paul's partner on the second missionary journey, opposition did not discourage him (Acts 17:1–4). Silas participated in exciting situations. Along with Paul, he planted the first church in Thessalonica. He felt the pain of being flogged (Acts 16:22–23). He sang praises to God in a Philippian jail. He heard the threatening shouts of city officials in Thessalonica, "These men who have caused trouble all over the world have now come here" (Acts 17:6).

• Jason represents one of many people who opened their homes to visiting evangelists. Jason's part to spread the gospel was to welcome Paul and Silas to Thessalonica. Being their host, Jason took a lot of flak from the city officials (Acts 17:5–9).

• Lydia, a prominent merchant, opened her home to the missionaries. Her part was to offer prayer support and the comfort of her home.

• Luke, a Gentile, combined the care of the body and the care of the soul. An educated physician with a passion to witness, Luke was an attentive traveling companion for Paul. His interest in historical detail preserved his personal experiences with Jesus and the movement of the Holy Spirit through the Book of Acts.

• Titus, a Greek believer, was trained by Paul to organize and lead churches. Accompanying Paul to Jerusalem, he stood before the church as an example of what Christ was doing among the Gentiles.

Paul sent Titus to Corinth to deal with church difficulties. To Paul's delight, Titus and the Corinthians developed affection for one another (2 Cor. 7:13–14; 8:16).

Sent as Paul's special representative to Crete, Titus lived among the Cretans who referred to themselves as "liars, evil brutes, lazy gluttons." Paul trusted Titus to minister in a very difficult place. As a responsible, loving leader, Titus dug in his heels and strengthened the church in Crete.

• Priscilla and Aquila met Paul in Corinth after they had been expelled from Rome because of an anti-Semitic decree. Being tentmakers, they began a business in the agora. Being Jews they attended the synagogue. Because of these two common interests, they furnished Paul a livelihood and lodging. Returning to Rome at the end of their expulsion, they hosted one of the house churches (Rom. 16:3–5).

PART AND PARCEL
Phoebe, a Servant in the Church

Phoebe's life was dedicated to aiding the sick and the poor in Cenchreae, Corinth. Paul called her "my friend." On hearing that Phoebe was traveling to Rome, Paul asked her to take a letter to the house churches.

Tucked away in Phoebe's satchel was a letter written by Paul to "all God's beloved in Rome." Entrusted to Phoebe was a theological treatise providing a comprehensive explanation of the gospel. The letter was passed around the house churches.

Power-conscious citizens listened when Paul wrote that the gospel, God's power, could change lives.

Slaves listened when Paul referred to himself as a slave of Christ—yet possessing complete freedom.

All classes listened when Paul wrote that the gospel was offered freely to everyone.

The Jewish community struggling to reach God through rituals listened as Paul announced that faith in Christ justifies individuals before God.

This truth echoes down through the years. One day spiritually troubled Martin Luther understood the significance of "the just shall live by faith." God's grace as a gift became the motivating force in his life.

Phoebe carried in her satchel a proclamation that centuries later produced the Protestant Reformation.

Today when you and I rest secure in our salvation through faith in Christ; when we feel His power surge through our minds and emotions; when we experience freedom in servanthood, we might pause to appreciate Paul who wrote the letter, the Roman Christians who treasured the letter, the Holy Spirit Who protected it through persecution, and Paul's helper Phoebe—all accomplishing their part in God's plan.

Paul could have paid the same tribute to all his friends as he did to Priscilla and Aquila: "Fellow workers in Christ Jesus. . . . They risked their lives for me. Not only I but also all the churches of the Gentiles are grateful to them (Rom. 16:3–4).

MY PART
My Cluster Has Preparation Pieces

In retrospect we understand that a lasting effort requires extensive preparation. Recall various life experiences that influenced your part in God's plan, such as education or training, recreational activities, hobbies, crises, and church involvement.

At the beginning of my husband's and my ministry, I felt a restlessness to discover a personal ministry. Beneath the consolation of involvement in various ministries, the uneasiness gnawed.

Time passed. In response to a harried mother's plea, I reluctantly met Beth, an unwed, pregnant teenager. The first hug melted my prejudice and her suspicions. I promised to be with Beth during the delivery. But I felt it was only an interruption in my diligent search for a ministry.

The same week that I met Beth, I enrolled in a literacy workshop. Teaching nonreaders must be my personal ministry, I thought. Then the unthinkable happened. Beth's labor interrupted the second day of training. I was angry with myself for a promise, at Beth for early labor, at God for His timing, and at the closed door precluding a literacy ministry.

Roaming the maternity wing during the hours of Beth's labor, I held the hands of children having babies. At twilight, wrenched with emotion, I sputtered to the Lord, "I don't know how You plan to work this out; but my life will be inextricably bound to teenagers like those I met today, won't it?"

For months, I had sought a personal ministry. In the brevity of ten hours, the Lord closed one door but gave me a peek at the possibilities through a crack in another one. My experience is that "his paths are beyond tracing out" (Rom. 11:33).

In our second pastorate, the crack in my door to ministry increased to a wedge. Accepting an invitation from a youth consultant, I led human sexuality seminars at the state conference center for three summers. I became comfortable verbalizing facts and feelings about sex among Christian youth.

In our third church, the door opened. As a result of our group's study of juvenile delinquency, I became a volunteer with the juvenile court. The intense training emphasized accepting the youth as persons. A flashback: Beth and the girls in the hospital having babies taught me acceptance.

The training detailed major problems of delinquents. Sex topped the list. A flashback: The seminars prepared me to communicate without intimidation or embarrassment.

I followed the probation officer into the cubicle to meet my first probationer. Rage tensed her body and stared through eyes riveted to the ceiling, intent on ignoring me. The cubicle door was the entrance to a ministry and an exit for my restlessness.

Some of our best experiences come without advance knowledge. God lovingly leads in spite of our anger, uncertainty, or vagueness. Doors open. We walk through, relying on God's decisions. In retrospect, the path that led me into the court is clear. But on the walk toward it, only faith recognized God's activity.

Retrospection deepens our humility, excites love, and stimulates trust and obedience. A warning is that we must guard against recalling the past as a way to nourish pride. However, remembering in order to find traces of God's graciousness results in "joy and gladness . . . thanksgiving and the sound of singing" (Isa. 51:3).

• How are your personality traits maturing rather than completely changing?

• Do you have a trait you consider a weakness? Ask the Lord to discipline the trait to use for His glory. God made you as you are in order to use you as He planned.

"In the meantime" is a significant interval in God's timing. Simultaneously, as the Lord prepares you, He is also leading others and guiding circumstances to help you accomplish your part.

To discover my part in God's plan is not simple because the Lord is not only dealing with me, He is also dealing with you. And my part must harmonize with your part in His plan. Prayer for one another is crucial.

• Think of people who crossed your path as if by chance, yet they rescued your sanity by assisting you make a decision, clear a hurdle, endure a difficulty, ease your stress, or laugh at yourself.

• How have instances of no apparent purpose blessed your relationships, your ministries, your spiritual growth, your understanding of yourself?

One telephone conversation introduced me to missions involvement. Mrs. Harvey Haggard was fulfilling her part in God's plan as an extraordinary missions leader. In the meantime, I married a minister who was called to a church in the county where Mrs. Haggard lived. Because of her hospitable nature, Maggie Haggard called to welcome the new pastor's family. Neither she nor I recognized her call as initiating God's plan for my life.

Her kindnesses continued through many months. A sense of duty, not interest, motivated me to attend missions meetings she planned. Her life intersected mine when I was searching for a purpose to make a difference in the world. I had read an appealing statement by William Menninger: "It is a mental health practice to find a mission that is so much bigger than you are that you can never accomplish it alone, a mission for the common good, a task that takes thought and energy."[4] I never had thought of missions involvement as fulfilling Menninger's criteria for a healthy personality. I totally had dismissed Woman's Missionary Union® (WMU®) as an option to find my part in God's plan.

My indifference to Maggie's interest in missions did not deter her nurturing nature. Because I enjoyed her company, I accepted her invitation to attend a retreat at the WMU camp. She suggested that I "pay attention" to everything I saw and heard.

In retrospect, this is what happened: When I entered the camp, the world for me was a dark globe suspended in space. When I left, a colorful world (red, yellow, black, and white; precious in God's sight) was in my heart.

Recently I sent Maggie a birthday card with the message: "Happy birthday to someone who made a beautiful difference in my life."

Through the years, she has continued to mentor me. Her most recent keepsake note read: "Hi. Today is the day you will be elected Alabama's state WMU president. I'm so glad. And I will pray for you. Remember when God calls, He makes a way."

A telephone call that seemed insignificant launched a love for God's world that deepens every day.

"So it has gone from the start, God using one to influence another. Maybe one of the joys of heaven will be the gathering up of the threads of influence and tracing them in all their ramifications."[5]

[1]William Sanford LaSor, *Men Who Knew Christ* (Glendale, CA: Regal Books, 1971), 90–91.
[2]Charles F. Pfeiffer and Howard F. Vos, *The Wycliffe Historical Geography of Bible Lands* (Chicago: Moody Press, 1967), 247–52.
[3]William J. Fallis, *Studies in Acts* (Nashville: Broadman Press, 1949), 71.
[4]Bernard H. Hall and Richard Rhodes, eds., *Living in a Troubled World* (Kansas City, MO: Hallmark Editions, 1967), 53.
[5]Washington Bryan Crumpton, *A Book of Memories 1842–1920* (Montgomery, AL: Baptist Mission Board, 1921), 160.

5

GOD'S PLAN *To Energize the Church*

MY PART *To Submit to His Power*

"For this reason I remind you to fan into flame the gift of God, which is in you through the laying on of my hands. For God did not give us a spirit of timidity but a spirit of power, of love, and of self-discipline" *(2 Tim. 1:6–7).*

The "Tempting Sweets" puzzle filled with chocolate pieces lured the children away from their age-appropriate puzzles of dinosaurs.

Many of the pieces were similar in shape, causing a small child to mistake one piece for another. And so without supervision, the children jammed together pieces in a mismatched jumble. A casual glance at the puzzle did not reveal the misplaced pieces. We discovered the chaos as we attempted to interlock additional pieces. The completed picture depended on the correct placement of pieces.

Attempting to put together the pieces of our part in God's plan without His supervision throws life into disorder. God is good not to leave us floundering to find His will. Through His Holy Spirit, He gives us grace gifts enabling us to do our part. The Holy Spirit also helps us cultivate Christ's qualities (Gal. 5:22–23) that define our behavior as we use our gifts.

PUZZLE PIECE
Imagine Paul in a Roman Dungeon

I once stood in a subterranean dungeon of the Mamertine Prison in Rome where Paul was confined before his martyrdom. Cold, rough rocks formed the walls, and dampness chilled the chamber. The city sewer system ran past the outer wall and seeped through the porous rock. Aware of the dungeon's condition, I shuddered for Paul when he requested Timothy to bring his cloak and to come before winter (2 Tim. 4:13,21).

When Paul was imprisoned, only a hole in the ceiling admitted light, air, and prisoners who were dropped through it into the cell. Paul lived in the prison for at least two years. From the cell he wrote his last letter to Timothy. Imagine Paul hunched over a wobbly table placed under the hole in the ceiling where the narrow stream of light focused on the parchment.

Paul realized that his death was imminent (2 Tim. 4:6). He had spent time and energy discipling Timothy to pastor a generation of people who had not seen Jesus. Paul knew that the ministry would challenge Timothy's abilities. Perhaps intuitively Paul detected a slight deficiency in courage when Timothy faced the intimidation of the Corinthian believers. Maybe Timothy had not boldly expressed disapproval at the offending actions of the believers. Because of Timothy's inexperience, Paul might have felt an uneasiness to leave Timothy with fearful responsibilities.

So Paul wrote, "To Timothy, my dear son" (2 Tim. 1:2). Paul's affectionate salutation was tinged with solemnity.

Lonely in the dungeon, he expressed his yearning to see
Timothy. He remembered Timothy's tears when their
ministries sent them in different directions. Paul recalled
Timothy's ordination when he received his spiritual
gift(s).

Paul felt joy for Timothy's faith and his Christian heritage. The faith that lived in his grandmother and his
mother was now at home with him.

PUZZLE PIECE
Imagine Paul Laying His Hands on Timothy

Paul met Timothy in Lystra on his second missionary
journey (Acts 16:1). Timothy's trust in God and excellent
reputation in the community impressed Paul. A child of
mixed marriage, Timothy's mother, Eunice, was a Jew;
his father, a Greek. Lois, Timothy's grandmother, and
Eunice influenced Timothy's interest in God by teaching
him the Scriptures (2 Tim. 1:5).

Philippians 2:19–24 records Paul's high regard for
Timothy. Being like-minded, Paul trusted Timothy to
interpret situations as he would. Paul sent Timothy to
handle difficult moral, doctrinal, and administrative
problems in the Corinthian church. Possibly Timothy's
youth and inexperience aggravated the situation, and he
was ineffectual in solving the problems.

Paul still trusted Timothy even though the Corinthians rebuffed him (1 Cor. 4:17) and sent him to oversee
the work in Ephesus. That city was another difficult place
where citizens hostile to Christianity worshiped the goddess Diana.

As a close associate, Timothy accompanied Paul on his
second and third missionary journeys. He was with Paul
during his first Roman imprisonment (Col. 1:1). Much
later Timothy was imprisoned and released (Heb. 13:23).

PUZZLE PIECE
Imagine Timothy Reading Paul's Last Letter

The environment in Ephesus where Timothy labored to mature a congregation of believers contrasted with Paul's bleak condition in Rome. Imagine Timothy excitedly reaching for the letter extended to him by the circuit's hired runner (today's postal worker).

Dodging the crowds of citizens and elbowing past throngs of international traders and tourists, Timothy exited the city limits of Ephesus through the Magnesian Gate. Climbing a slope, he sat in the shade of a lush vineyard. In the valley below the sight of Ephesus mesmerized him as it did everyone entering the city from the East. With the sun striking the white marble structures, overlaid with gold and decorated with brightly painted frescoes, Ephesus twinkled like a precious gem.

In the distance the 60-foot-high columns of Diana's temple cast long, ominous shadows down the slope toward the city. Perhaps within sight of the epitome of paganism, Timothy unrolled the scroll and read, "To Timothy, my dear son."

Although encouragement punctuates the letter, a somber tone weaves through Paul's advice to Timothy. The letter reiterates Paul's priorities for mainstay: well-grounded doctrine, unwavering faith, power to bear difficulties, and enduring love.

PUZZLE PIECE
Imagine a Flame

Despondent by Paul's imprisonment and pressured from trying to pastor believers badgered by Diana's devotees, Timothy's personal fears could have smothered the fire of his faith. Encouraging Timothy to be faithful, Paul exhorted him "to fan into flame the gift of God."

Timothy was not exhorted to stir up his natural or acquired abilities or his enthusiasm. The fire to rekindle and to keep burning was God's gift within him. At this ordination, Timothy received the gift(s) of the Spirit for his particular ministry qualifying him for his part in God's plan. These gifts equip all believers to do our part in God's plan.

No doubt early in his missionary career, Paul realized that God built churches through individuals gifted in distinctive ways. Some new believers lived in Corinth. Still clinging to Corinthian ethics, they were greedy, gluttonous, and factious. Yet they formed a church.

Several hundred miles away in Rome new believers lived in a city obsessed with power, patriotism, and gory sports events. When Christians shared, "Jesus is Lord," the pagan citizens shouted, "Caesar is Lord." Yet they formed a church.

When Paul preached in Ephesus, many people who had lost their sense of decency in a vulgar society responded to the gospel. They formed a church and changed their society.

How could new believers from pagan backgrounds form churches? God generously gave those first Christians every necessary spiritual gift to minister and witness in a decadent society. He gave every necessary resource to build a church in a pagan culture.

PUZZLE PIECE
Imagine Different Kinds of Churches

God designed His spiritual body with certain needs. The needs of today are the same as in the first century. The same gifts that enabled the first-century churches to survive and thrive are available to us today. The Holy Spirit assigns gifts and correctly places people to meet needs in your church. Notice which gift meets a specific need:

Speaking Gifts

Need	Gift
A climate in which people can hear God's call	Apostolic
Preaching God's word	Prophecy
Instruction	Teaching
Reaching the lost	Evangelism
Encouragement	Exhortation
Information	Knowledge
Relate knowledge to life	Wisdom

Serving Gifts

Need	Gift
Support	Helps or serving
Fellowship	Hospitality
Financial support	Giving
Direction	Government, administration, leadership
Doing kind deeds	Mercy
Power	Faith
Protection	Discernment

Spiritual gifts are God's primary means of accomplishing His plan to seek and to save the lost. His plan depends on our belief that we have a gift and on our trust in His placement of us. Our unique gifts become resources for helping spread the gospel message. They open opportunities for us to share our faith and to change our society. When we allow the Holy Spirit to supervise the use of gifts(s), the pieces of life's puzzle shape up. Consider these needs and how God can use our gifts to meet them

Perhaps on a cold winter morning you have shivered before a fireplace uncovering coals from the night before. You carefully applied kindling and blew until the flame appeared. This is the picture Paul described. All fires die unless from time to time they are stirred. A motivation for reigniting the gift's flame is to remember our Lord did not say He would spit us out for being hot or cold but for being lukewarm (Rev. 3:16).

Peter's reminder to serve "with the strength that God provides" (1 Peter 4:11) is applicable to all the gifts. While each of us is required to use our gifts within our abilities, God does not expect ministry beyond our abilities. We burn out rather than flame up when we dabble in gifts not assigned to us. Paul's personal testimony was "never be lacking zeal, but keep your spiritual fervor, serving the Lord" (Rom. 12:11).

Sometimes we ask the wrong question about our part in God's plan. We ask, "Who am I, O God, that I could ever be important to You? What do I have to offer?"

The real question is instead, Who are You, O God, Who would pour divine grace into my clay vessel, Who blessed my life with a gift empowering me to have a part in sharing Your grace, Who is longsuffering when my flame flickers?

In the distance, I heard a roll of thunder. Clouds gathered, the winds blew, rain pelted the study window, and lightning flashed occasionally. Gradually, the winds increased to a roar beating torrents of rain against the window. Suddenly a deafening explosion and flashes of blue and yellow light knocked me to the floor. Abruptly an eerie silence stunned the senses. Moaning, I crawled to the window. Peering between specks of melted bark splashed against the pane, I saw spiral streaks like finger indentions circling two oak trees. When the storm subsided, I tiptoed to the trees and traced the pattern of God's omnipotent finger.

O God, I like to feel the soothing touch of Your hand. But I beg to feel the fire of Your finger.

PUZZLE PIECE
Imagine a Mob Surrounding Paul

Paul and Timothy lived in a society hostile to Christians and the church. Timothy had cause to fear physically. He had seen Paul stoned, bleeding, and left for dead in Lystra (Acts 14:19). Romans who had crucified Jesus controlled the politics in all the provinces.

Travel was hazardous. Sea travelers sailed on cargo vessels because passenger ships were nonexistent. Besides storms causing treacherous seas, ships, hard to maneuver, wrecked frequently.

Roman highways were adequate for pedestrian traffic, but robbers were a constant danger.

In addition to fearful circumstances, Timothy's timid natural disposition neutralized his courage. His gentle spirit was in danger of being cowed by forceful unbelievers. In fact, Paul had warned the Corinthians not to scare Timothy. "See to it that he has nothing to fear while he is with you"; and "No one . . . should refuse to accept him" (1 Cor. 16:10–11).

Frayed edges of jigsaw puzzle pieces do not fit together smoothly. In like manner, frazzle-edged experiences in life's puzzle generate uneasy feelings, anxious thoughts, and concerns. Human frailties tend to unravel us.

Paul struggled with a chronic physical problem that hindered his work.

Paul had relationship problems; his disagreement with Barnabas about John Mark is one example.

When faith and life seem to disagree, depend on Psalm 37:23–24 (CEV): "If you do what the Lord wants, he will make certain each step you take is sure. The Lord will hold your hand, and if you stumble, you still won't fall."

PUZZLE PIECE
Imagine Thick, Rusty Chains

Do you own a chain necklace among your jewelry pieces? We wear everything from expensive silver to four-leaf clover chains. We wear short, long, and double chains with round, oblong, or square links. I even have a paper-clip chain necklace—a keepsake from a child. All kinds of chains adorn us.

Paul was familiar with chains. He called them shackles, not adornments. He was chained to dungeon walls and to soldiers' wrists because of power-hungry people's fears that Paul's leadership would topple the status quo.

The Latin root for the word *timid* is "to fear." Timidity is defined as always being ready to be afraid of anything new, different, uncertain, or unknown.

Today, fears, like invisible chains, hinder our usefulness. Many are similar to the fears of Paul and Timothy, only tweaked a mite because of society's differences. Links in the chain of fear that imprison us include opinion of the majority who oppose God's standards, defeatist attitudes, destructive habits, sensuality, inordinate

62

ambitions, injustices, burdens because of calamities, oppressive relationships, and greed.

When fear controls, we never attempt tasks beyond business as usual. Fear results from seeing obstacles and opponents to God's plan more clearly than seeing God.

PUZZLE PIECE
<u>Imagine an Explosion</u>

When the Holy Spirit entrusted us with grace gifts to do our parts in God's plan, He did not shove us into the community saying, "Good luck" or "Do the best you can." He equipped us with strength to do our parts. The antidote for fear is power, love, and self-control.

God energizes members of His body with His power: "And how very great is his power at work in us who believe. This power working in us is the same as the mighty strength which he used when he raised Christ from death and seated him at his right side in the heavenly world" (Eph. 1:19–20 TEV). The Holy Spirit is our actual strength, not a supplement for human energy.

The words *dynamite* and *dynamic* originate in the New Testament word for power. Jesus promised an explosive power. The description of the expanding outburst of the early church is exciting (Acts 4:32–36). Luke records that "with great power the apostles continued to testify to the resurrection of the Lord Jesus, and much grace was upon them all (Acts 4:33).

The word *great* in the Greek language is *megas*. Today, scientists use the word as a measurement for power. One megaton is equal to the explosive force of 1 million tons of dynamite. With *megas* in mind, reread Acts 4:33: "And with a million tons of power the apostles continued to testify to the resurrection of the Lord and a million tons of grace were upon them all." If a million tons of physical power detonated over the world, life would not continue as usual. If a million tons of spiritual power released a million tons of grace, "every knee should bow and every tongue confess that Jesus Christ is Lord to the glory of God the Father" (Phil. 2:10–11).

God's plan is to seek and to save the lost. Our part in God's plan is to be a releaser of great grace!

PUZZLE PIECE
Imagine a Heart

In his second letter to Timothy, Paul mentioned two of Christ's qualities. The first was love. Paul wrote to the Colossians, "And over these virtues put on love, which binds them all together in perfect unity" (Col. 3:14). Love is the inner disposition that produces the other fruit. The reciprocal love that God has for us and we have for God finds an outward expression in loving people (Matt. 22:37–40).

What kind of love should motivate the gifts and control our relationships? Paul did not define an abstract idea. Instead, he featured feelings that are apt to produce clashes among people and described how love would act. Love in action is
- never inconsiderate, critical, or intolerant;
- content with its opportunities, abilities, possessions, and position;
- not boastful;
- never rude, always courteous, and tactful;
- never insistent on its own way;
- never touchy or bad-tempered; never angry at personal hurt, only at injustice;
- never resentful;
- never slanderous.

(1 Cor. 13:4–7)

In 1 Corinthians 13, Paul painted a word picture of Jesus. Love is Christlikeness. Our likeness to Christ is proportionate to our love for others.

In 1 Peter 4:8, Peter described active love as exerting and stretching itself to the limit of endurance, much like a runner determined to win a race. Love demands our earnest effort. Earnest means undiluted. Earnest love cannot be weakened. We apply it full strength to those hard to love, to those who harass, to those who would take our lives. Earnest love causes us to be gentle with the weaknesses in other people, hide faults, and patiently suffer the unkind actions of others.

For the most part, biblical love refers to attitudes and actions that seek the best for others regardless of our natural inclinations. A sole emphasis on love as an act of will gives the impression that godlike love lacks emotion. Writing to persecuted believers in Asia Minor, Peter used expressions as "love one another deeply, from the heart" (1 Peter 1:22) and "love as brothers" (1 Peter 3:8). Paul's advice to the Roman Christians was "Be devoted to one another in brotherly love" (Rom. 12:10). These verses indicate that warm feelings of affection, similar to family love, are appropriate to accompany ministry through our gifts.

PUZZLE PIECE
Imagine a Runner in a Race

What causes undisciplined moments in your life? Responses to this question run the gamut, from my favorite easy chair to credit cards; from banana cream pie to television. One undisciplined moment can make the day uncomfortable or ruined. Think how constantly devastated is the totally undisciplined person. For many people, the lack of self-control is a way of life.

Paul mentioned self-control as a quality of Jesus. Disciplined energies affect every piece in life's cluster of puzzle pieces. Paul wrote that he was a prisoner of Jesus Christ by choice. He grasped the meaning of freedom in bondage. The free person is the one who is a prisoner of godly principles. The testimonies of people who seek freedom through excesses reveal the tragedies of their attempts for happiness. God created us with the potential for good or evil. We are not robots programmed for certain responses. We have free will to choose and then to share in the consequences of the decisions.

Self-discipline is the ability to control actions, feelings, and responses. It is habitual self-restraint, not sporadic moderation. Self-discipline is a personal trait. God deals with us as individuals. Different temptations appeal to different people. Your stumbling block might not be your neighbor's. Jesus taught us not to judge another's actions or reactions. Even so, when we get a vision of the Spirit's discipline, we are tempted to begin disciplining each other saying, "Why doesn't she do it this way?" or "If I were her, I would . . ." We cannot make rules for each other, but having rules to guide ourselves is crucial.

Chastisement is a form of discipline (Heb. 12:8–10). God's discipline has a gracious purpose. However, we feel the rod before we see the good results. Afflictions draw our attention to unforgiven sins. Chastenings convince us of moral carelessness.

Self-discipline also denotes sound judgment that allows us to distinguish between the good and the best. In times of stress, difficult situations, even persecutions, self-discipline helps us avoid hysteria. Sound judgment reminds us to behave sensibly instead of wavering between zealousness and indifference.

Discipline aids commitment. Lasting commitment rests on the will rather than the emotions. Surges of emotional feelings cannot be sustained indefinitely. Commitments are kept by a disciplined will.

Peter urges believers to "be clear minded and self-controlled so that you can pray" (1 Peter 4:7). A disciplined mind concentrates on deep yearnings. Life's distractions do not interrupt the prayers of a focused, self-controlled person. An alert pray-er has a keen sensitivity to specific needs.

Maturing Christians know that the most beneficial discipline comes from within, not without. Paul compares the strict regimen of an athlete to a Christian's training for life's competitions. Running aimlessly or fighting sloppily like beating the air is inept training for a race or a boxing match (1 Cor. 9:24–27). Applying the analogy to our spiritual lives, only serious training in practical holiness and self-denial will strengthen us for the race. The spirit of self-control enables us to run and not be weary. "Discipline . . . produces a harvest of righteousness and peace for those who have trained by it" (Heb. 12:11).

PART AND PARCEL
Missions Leader Par Excellence

Mary Essie Stephens "taught by example that God had given her a spirit of power, and of love, and of a sound mind," exclaimed Camilla Lowry.

Ministering alongside her in many capacities as a state missions leader, Camilla benefited by striving for the high standards set before her by Mary Essie Stephens.

Camilla remembers Mary Essie Stephens as:
- a quietly effective motivator and encourager helping others fulfill their tasks without taking credit for ideas and efforts;
- a noncomplainer, though she shouldered heavy family and denominational responsibilities;

- an unwavering supporter of missionaries through her prayers and sacrificial giving, through her life's work, through visits to missions fields;
- a team player who dealt with difficulties, kept confidences, and discussed only matters that would affect the work;
- a Christian loyal "to her Lord, to her church, to her family, to her job, to her own mentors, and to friends who shared the experiences of her life."

Mary Essie Stephens lived 2 Timothy 1:7 in practical application.

MY PART
My Cluster Includes Testifying to God's Grace

If for any reason the fire in your life has become a bed of coals instead of a blaze, stir up the gift of God! Consider these possibilities to help you:

•Identify your gift in one or more of the following ways:
  * Investigate the possibilities listed in 1 Corinthians 12:4–11, Romans 12:6–8, Ephesians 4:11–13, and 1 Peter 4:9–11.
  * Consider your desires and inclinations. What do you like to do? We gravitate toward areas of interest. The possibility is that we use our gift(s) naturally without realizing that the activity originates through our gift(s).
  * Consider needs or problems that concern you. Do you see the hungry and think of ways to distribute food? Your gift is mercy.
  * Refrain from the tendency to disregard a gift because of its name. Prophecy sounds theological or pastoral, but laypersons minister through this gift also.

* Accept affirmation from other people about your gift. Accept compliments as expressions of gratitude for how your gift ministers to a need.
* Realize that ministries exercised through your gift result in joy, satisfaction, and excitement; not boredom or frustration.
* Pray. Christ desires members of His body to do their part in His plan. Ask Him!

What gift do you need to fan into flame?

How will your responses to these questions affect my part in God's plan?

• How much energy does your church expend on planning exciting programs to attract new members? Is it possible to become too programmed?

Does your church assess the needs then discern which gifted members will satisfy the needs?

Do you trust the Holy Spirit to call members to ministries?

Are you suspicious of any spontaneous activity of the Holy Spirit that interrupts rigid agendas?

Can you explain all of your church's busyness in human terms? Is everything you do the result of human effort?

• In deciding your part in God's plan do you inquire about God's mind in the matter or act on your impulses?

What has God's power accomplished in your life since you accepted Jesus as Savior?

• Read 1 Corinthians 13, Romans 12:9–13, and Ephesians 4:25–32. Decide which behaviors need improvement in your life.

If any of the verses convict you of lack of love, confess your failure, then decide to live in loving ways indicated in the verses. Ask the Lord to make your love increase and overflow for each other (1 Thess. 3:12).

• Read the important promise in 1 Corinthians 10:13. Remember the last time you were tempted to resist God's plan?

What was the way or who was the person provided for escape?

How did you take advantage of the provision?

What needs discipline in your life? Tongue? Thoughts? Bible study? Prayer? Ministry? Eating habits? Temper? Work? Recreation? Other?

Dell Scoper's advice will ignite the flame: "The only way one can respond to the pressures of life with power, love, and self-control is to be steady and secure at the center. This does not happen overnight; but happens only by a daily, sustained, top-priority time with the Lord Jesus."

With our gifts flaming, with fears banished, with Christ's qualities evident in our behavior, we will boldly testify of God's grace!

6

GOD'S PLAN — *To Do Good*
MY PART — *To Live God's Good-ness*

"The Lord God has told us what is right and what he demands: 'See that justice is done, let mercy be your first concern, and humbly obey your God'" (Mic. 6:8 CEV).

"Be kind and compassionate to one another (Eph. 4:32).

We put the "Tempting Sweets" puzzle together by different methods. Now and then we all sat together but worked independently. At times one person worked alone assembling a complete cupcake before adding it to the larger puzzle. Other times two people helped each other connect pieces of divinity icing on the medallion cookies. Cooperating while using different methods we steadily progressed assembling the puzzle. At all times we compared our progress with the illustration on the box.

God's plan is to seek and to save the lost. Ministry offers us occasions to be a part of this plan by helping meeting peoples' needs and in the process sharing the gospel with them. To be vital, ministry must be an inner experience of righteousness and tenderness not merely an action. "To do" religious activities is much simpler than "to be" persons God desires. To be God's helper requires fair treatment in a spirit of reconciliation; a delight in every opportunity to do good—not only showing mercy but also loving mercy; and a submissive dependence on God.

Our guide, the Bible, emphasizes our responsibility to minister to one another. The Old Testament law dealt with society's problems of drunkenness, crime, corrupt government, economic injustice, prostitution, unsanitary conditions, and inadequate diet (Lev. 18; 19; Deut. 19; 24). It also dealt with people who had special needs: orphans, widows, poor, strangers, divorcees, aged, sick, and hungry (Ex. 22:25–27; Lev. 14: 21–32; Deut. 15:1–11). An instance in Isaiah 58:6–10 reminds us of an advocacy ministry by standing between people in crisis and the "finger-pointing, malicious talking community." The prophets spoke out that God's primary concern was not related to extravagant rituals, but to acts of justice, mercy, and love.

Christian ethics are founded on the life and teachings of Christ. His merciful compassion to seek and to save the lost caused Him to identify with the needs of the total person. Jesus offered His ministry to the physical and spiritual needs of people as proof to John the Baptist that He was the Messiah (Matt. 11:4–5).

To understand the extent of God's love for people we need only look to the Cross. In the Cross, we find our pattern for ministry: a love-motivated concern for the whole person demonstrated in a voluntary sacrifice. We must take advantage of every opportunity to minister whether by individual effort or by action in combination with others.

PUZZLE PIECE
Imagine Your Gift Helping One Person

After learning about the high recidivism rate of youth offenders, I vented my frustration to the probation officer. "Why bother to help kids change direction knowing that within a few months they will return to their delinquent lifestyle?"

Mr. Osborne listened patiently before replying. "You cannot change the trend of delinquency in the United States, in this state, or in this city. But you can make a difference on the street where you live."

Do moments of compassion so motivate you to minister that you fling open your door with outstretched arms to embrace the world? But the crush of hurting humanity overwhelms compassion. The futility of soothing all the sorrow slams the door! Quickly crack the door and look just on the street where you live.

Within God's plan are ways for one person to minister. The empowered body of Christ does not move en masse. We circulate separately through our communities where the Holy Spirit nudges us into ministries rooted in our gifts. The gifted administrator volunteered in the office of the human resources professional. The gifted exhorter answered phones for the suicide hot line. The gifted helper stocked the hospital's intensive care waiting room with small pillows and hygiene supplies. In the same waiting room, the one with the gift of mercy fluffed the pillows and listened to sad details of sickness and surgeries. Ministering gifts open opportunities to share our faith.

On Thanksgiving Eve, a line of shoppers waited outside the supermarket for grocery carts. Once inside, the binge buyers and gourmet cooks, searching for that special ingredient, jockeyed for positions at the shelves. In a

74

line of bumper-to-bumper carts, I crept down the aisle. In the surreal scene of harried people moving in slow motion, I saw her. The woman with the pensive expression pushed an empty cart.

"You must be caught in the traffic of a wrong aisle," I said, nodding toward her cart.

"No," she sighed. "Every holiday eve I come to the grocery store to enjoy the crowd. Holidays are lonely for people who are alone."

Ministry involves being Jesus' friendly presence to people isolated in bumper-to-bumper housing or work cubicles and to those who have no one awaiting them at home.

Ministry also involves listening and encouraging, which require time and attention—difficult to give consistently. Paul wrote of Timothy, "I have no one else like him, who takes a genuine interest in your welfare" (Phil. 2:20). He adds an incriminating observation, "For everyone looks out for his own interests not those of Jesus Christ" (Phil. 2:21).

The probation officer reported that the halfway house for ex-offenders had ample supplies of furniture, food, and money. He said, "The women need friends to acclimate them back into society. Would you miss your church one Sunday to accompany an ex-offender to the church in the community where she will live? Would you help her budget her meager income? Would you step from behind the sacks of groceries and checkbooks and offer yourself?"

PART AND PARCEL
Ministering at a Mobile-Home Park

"I would pass by the mobile-home park on my way to and from work each day," Kristy Carr recalls. "I began to think of the people living in those mobile homes. I knew the statistics—90 percent of the residents in most multi-housing areas are unchurched. As the days went by, I began to ask myself who was ministering to these people. After a while, I began to convince myself that the local churches were certainly meeting their needs. Since there were two, possibly three, churches within walking distance of the mobile-home park, I was sure that these churches were meeting their needs—both physical and spiritual. I had met several of the children who reside in the mobile-home park because they attend the same school as my children. I had opportunities to talk with some of them while eating lunch with my own children in the school cafeteria. Many have had difficulties learning English, as many of the families in the mobile-home park are Hispanic.

"The summer of 1999, my husband and I, along with 60 other adults and youth from our church, had the opportunity to travel to Brasilia, Brazil, on a missions trip to work with missionary Ida Mae Hays. When I returned home, I was so excited about what we had just experienced in Brazil. This was certainly one of those mountaintop experiences that keeps you going for a while. I continued to pass the mobile-home park each day and for a while was still convinced that the area churches were meeting their needs.

"However, I became so burdened for the people in the mobile-home park. I knew that the only way I would know for sure if any ministries were being done was to contact the area churches. After some calls, I soon found that at that time there were no churches making a concerted effort to reach these residents.

"I then realized that I not only needed to take opportunities to tell others about Jesus in other countries but also my own. I had the wonderful experience of being a part of Vacation Bible School in Brazil. Why not here in my own community? So my family, along with two teenagers, and I lead Friends Club. I also asked a friend, Carole, to be Pepito. Pepito is a wonderful puppet loved by all the girls and boys. The wonderful thing about Pepito is that he is bilingual. Since the Friends Club began, we have been able to have a health fair as well as a back-to-school party for the children. During these times we have been able to tell these children about Jesus and His love for them. We continue to find ways to cultivate relationships with these precious people. While giving the back-to-school party, we learned that a local church has begun English-as-a-second-language class for the residents. We are excited about partnering with this church and all other believers to tell everyone in this mobile-home park of Jesus and His love for them."

Kristy's part led her to an awareness and a response to a community need.

PUZZLE PIECE
Imagine Using Your Gift in a Group Ministry

Some ministries require the cooperation of individuals networking with community agencies.

After a nine-month study of juvenile delinquency, a group of women decided to become involved with solutions to the problem in our city. With suggestions from the chief probation officer, we got busy. Every Saturday a few women bought clothes, books, and games at yard sales to stock the detention center's closets and shelves. A cosmetologist trimmed hair and filed and painted nails. A teacher led Bible studies. Two retirees offered grandparent stability to the detained youth. As a group, we hosted seasonal parties. "I don't think I've ever eaten homemade candy," Joyce mused, as she folded marshmallow cream into the chocolate. Joyce and others in the detention center learned to make fudge after the group furnished the ingredients, assisted in the process, and listened to girls talk about houses that were not homes and women who were not mothers. Verbalizing calmed their hurts.

Though I received the training to become a court volunteer who could spend time with delinquent youth outside the center, Polly's contribution made possible my participation in the volunteer program. Polly's situation prevented her from involvement at the detention center. However, she asked to keep my three children any time I needed to be alone with a probationer friend. Polly taught me the meaning of "laboring together with God."

In the group we worked independently and together with a common goal of remedying circumstances of juvenile delinquents.

PUZZLE PIECE
Imagine Christian Women's Job Corps

Women in your community have needs that Christian Women's Job Corps® (CWJC®) can eliminate. Burdened with low self-esteems, the women have no job skills, no hope. Some are homeless, abandoned, and frightened. Some are working in low-wage positions. They need to upgrade their skills to provide for their families.

CWJC is a ministry that combines practical training, relationship building, emotional healing, and spiritual growth. The curriculum includes life-skills and job-readiness training. The women gain self-respect and self-sufficiency.

As a part of her training to become a site coordinator, Linda Henry had to feed a family of four on $4.52 per day for a week. "This is what a family would have to spend on food for a whole day," Linda explained. Within the limits, Linda bought one dozen eggs, one pound of dry pinto beans, one pint of milk, one box of store-brand macaroni and cheese, and one box of grits.

"There wasn't even enough money left to buy a loaf of bread," Linda said. "That was a real eye-opener for me."

Linda explained that just relieving the material burdens, such as paying electric bills, repairing a car, or helping with groceries, isn't enough. "We don't want to give a handout. We want to go to the source of the problem."

Each site networks with existing programs. "If the CWJC cannot provide a service or meet the need of a participant, we know where to send her for the service," Linda said.

Each participant is paired with a volunteer mentor who assesses the needs and develops the means to meet them. If a participant is unable to get to classes or appointments, the mentor provides transportation.

The mentor works one-on-one with the participant. Together they pray and study the Bible, the first textbook the participant receives. The CWJC creates a safe and inviting place for women to learn about themselves, improve their skills, and receive Jesus as Savior.

Supporting and participating in a CWJC site is a way to do right, to delight in helping others, and share in God's plan.

PART AND PARCEL
Stacy and LeAnn, CWJC Participants

"Two years ago I found myself and my children out in the cold, so to speak. I separated from my husband of 12 years," recalls Stacy Williams. "I tried to keep my children and me as stable as possible by working night shifts on the weekends and ironing for my neighbors during the week.

"After being on a waiting list for a year, the kids and I were able to move into Section 8 housing. Shortly thereafter, by the recommendation of my counselor, I started classes at the Christian Women's Job Corps, where my counselor also taught.

"I was feeling inadequate, depressed, and unable to cope with my new situation and provide for my kids. Through this new, positive, Christian environment, I was able to regain my self-esteem, confidence in my abilities, and strength in the Lord!

"Through much prayer and faith, not to mention guidance from the teachers of CWJC, I finally saw a light at the end of the tunnel! That light was hope! I had set many goals for myself. I am now a college student. Something I never thought was possible has become reality.

"God has blessed my children and me in so many ways. I know now that what I had gone through in the past was all in God's plan. Something bigger and better is waiting for my kids and me. And I know that as long as I allow the Lord to take control, I can go anywhere!"

At a surprise reception in her honor, Stacy received the national Sybil Bentley Dove Award. Stacy was described as "an outstanding student who had perfect attendance at class and is a focused and goal-oriented achiever who sets high standards and goals for herself." Her mentor's commendation affirmed Stacey's efforts: "Stacy is a self-motivated person who balances home, school, and work with a positive attitude—never fails to give God the credit."

Stacy plans to continue her education to become a radiology technician.

LeAnn Cook feels empowered by her participation in Christian Women's Job Corps. "I am a single mom with one child. I was very controlled in my marriage. He did not like what I wore or what I dressed my daughter in. He did not like the way I did anything and said I was not good enough.

"When my marriage came to an end and he was involved with another woman, I thought I had failed. I felt like a failure in my marriage relationship, my job, and my friends. I did not feel good about myself at all. I just wanted to hide in a corner and I cried a lot. I finally realized that crying was getting me nowhere, so I got off of my dusty-rusty and tried to find help. My daughter and I became involved in our church and we started to meet new friends. But I still didn't feel good about myself and knew this was not enough.

"That is when I met Elizabeth and she told me about Christian Women's Job Corps. The decision to be a part of this ministry saved my life. It means the world to me. When I first got into the program, I didn't know what to expect. But as I got more involved, I realized that the people there were sincere and truly cared about my daughter and me.

"Before CWJC, it was constantly up and down. My feelings were a roller coaster. After Elizabeth assigned me a mentor, I began to learn things. She has helped me feel good about myself and has taught me to set goals and work toward them. I have learned to achieve those goals through encouragement of others. She has taught me to put God first and trust Him in my life.

"As my daughter and I got involved in the Family Ministry, we learned how to focus on our family more. I learned to cut off the TV and have family time and family devotionals. My daughter has really enjoyed these times. She gets mad at me when I am tired or need to study. We are now doing this every night before we go to bed. If I forget, believe me, she lets me know! We have also learned to set goals for my daughter. She is doing very well. We both are doing journal writing. This helps us get out our feelings in writing before we say something we shouldn't. After a while, we go back and read what we wrote to see how far we have come.

"We love the Celebrations and Family Activity Days. They have helped us to feel good about ourselves and taught us to focus on our family, to work as a team, and to trust God. I don't know where my daughter and I would be today without CWJC. I believe the love and encouragement and having a mentor are the things that have changed not only my life but also my daughter's."

LeAnn adds, "As I was reading in my devotional, I came across a part about mentoring. It said, 'It's more than being friends, more than learning or teaching. Woman-to-woman mentoring helps women grow in their faith as they share life experiences.' It also said, 'While God's Word should always be our guiding light, mature Christian women who live godly lives can prove to be a refreshing source of wisdom and encouragement.' I believe this is true. I believe that putting a mentor with each person in CWJC is the key. It helps that person grow spiritually, mentally, and emotionally."

Life updates from former Christian Women's Job Corps participants inspire us to continue a profitable ministry.

Tammy Gaither came to the York County CWJC in Rock Hill, South Carolina, from a homeless shelter. The mother of one daughter, Tammy is a board member for the homeless shelter where she is also a motivational speaker to the women in the shelter. She is spokesperson for Habitat for Humanity, a speaker for CWJC, and a mentor in the ministry. Tammy has trained the mentors in the area of cultural diversity. She currently serves on the York County CWJC Board.

Active in her church, Tammy encourages other single parents through her Sunday School class. Training in English as a second language offers another opportunity to witness. When she spoke in her church about her life-changing experiences through CWJC, the televised service reached into many homes.

Elizabeth Ford, site coordinator for the York County CWJC, shares Bobbie Grant's update: "Bobbie graduated from York Technical College with a machine tool engineering degree. This traditional men's field pays well. Bobbie's well-paying job moved her on to self-sufficiency. She decided to start a cleaning business and to hire women who were struggling as she had. Bobbie knows the meaning of struggle—through college, paying debts, dealing with being a single parent. Yet she made it out of a downward cycle.

"She really has a fairy-tale ending to her struggle. She is engaged to a wonderful Christian man who helps her in her ministries at her church. He has purchased a four-bedroom home and a vehicle for them. He has been working with her three children in the areas of discipline, allowance, and family devotions. If we could write an ending for women involved in CWJC, we couldn't do this well!"

PART AND PARCEL
Serving as a Mentor

Laura Cook's friendship with Sheryl Barrett began at the CWJC site. God began preparing Laura for her part in ministry when she was a child. Her dad, a country doctor, followed the rural roads of the Appalachian Mountains ministering to the sick. As a volunteer, Laura's mother participated in local missions. Laura emphasized, "I saw missions at home." No doubt, her missions-minded family influenced Laura's career decision in nursing.

As a young adult, Laura's abusive marriage ended in divorce. Desiring to use her experience to give hope to others, Laura volunteered at a shelter for battered women. As Laura's situation changed, so did her involvement at the shelter. However, a social worker, knowing Laura's skills and interests, introduced her to CWJC where she became Sheryl's mentor.

Mentoring included practical details, such as helping Sheryl develop a plan and set reasonable goals to achieve a better life, learn to drive a car, earn a GED, and learn social skills. Encouragement is a key mentoring ingredient. With no family support, Sheryl appreciated Laura's motivating confidence in her abilities. Together they celebrated when Sheryl received her driver's license after three tries. They felt the joy of being Christian kin as Laura stood in the baptistery beside Sheryl during Sheryl's baptism.

Laura and Sheryl have a healthy friendship because they learn from each other. Laura has learned about

•love. Sheryl lives in a discouraging family environment. But with an amazing love she wants to work in order to provide for the family. Sheryl's love for people who disparage her motivates Laura to love fellow employees who do not know Jesus.

• generosity. Sheryl is willing to share from her meager income with those less fortunate. Noticing that a woman in the grocery line did not have money to buy all the items, Sheryl paid the difference.

• determination. Sheryl's resolve to accomplish her plan is worthy to emulate.

• worship. Laura led Sheryl to accept Jesus as Savior.

Her soul is warmed watching Sheryl vigorously sing praises to God.

• prayer. Throughout their friendship, Laura and Sheryl have prayed for God's intervention in Sheryl's life. The Lord has networked people to guide Sheryl in response to their prayers.

• dependence on God. Laura, with a lilt in her voice, exclaimed, "We are always looking to see what God is doing."

The mentoring relationship is vital for CWJC. Colossians 2:2 is an inspirational verse for mentors: "My purpose is that they may be encouraged in heart and united in love, so that they may have the full riches of complete understanding, in order that they may know the mystery of God, namely, Christ."

PUZZLE PIECE
Imagine a Scale of Justice

Twelve teenaged boys with a disrespectful swagger stood before Judge Barrow. Their stunned parents, cultured, influential citizens in the capital city, sat like stone statues in the courtroom.

After his reprimand for the seriousness of the crime, the judge asked each boy, "Why did you desecrate the graves in the city cemetery?"

The first boy responded with a nervous giggle, "We didn't have anything else to do."

Another admitted with a smirk, "Just 'cause we wanted to."

With a sideways glance at his buddies, one boy chortled, "We just wanted to have a little fun."

None of the boys showed any remorse for their crime spree.

Judge Barrow spoke decisively, "I am going to give you all the fun you can handle. For the duration of your probation, every day you will report to the city's cemetery crew. You will help maintain the property. You will assist in digging every grave. Your fun job will begin the reimbursement of the thousands of dollars you owe the city and the families of the deceased."

Gasps from the shocked parents echoed through the cavernous courtroom.

At the midway point of the boys' probation period, I returned to the court to hear the judge's assessment of their work in the cemetery. Standing erect before Judge Barrow, their tanned skin, toned muscles, and solemn demeanor indicated a change.

After reviewing the probation terms, the judge asked, "What do you have to say?"

One young man cleared his throat and stepped forward saying, "If it's OK with you, Judge Barrow, they (nodding toward the others) asked me to speak for all of us.

"Well, we agree that none of us will ever go into another cemetery until it's time to er . . . er . . . until we die. (The boys shook their heads.)

"We get lots of exercise. (The boys smiled.)

"Our probation officer let us meet some of the families of the folks whose graves we messed up. Some of them are poor—still paying on the stones we smashed. With our probation officer's help, we've decided to spend a couple of hours every week doing what we can for them. You know, like yard work or running errands— you know—just helping out."

That day in court I saw restorative justice.

I'll never forget Judge Barrow's expression. Still stern, his eyes twinkled a mite as he looked at each boy. Months before with creative sentencing, the judge decreed necessary punishment for a crime. The punishment set in motion a series of changes within the boys that restored them to contributing members of society.

The experience of the boys parallels biblical justice. A reflection of God's nature, biblical justice attempts to right wrongs and to find peaceful solutions to complaints and problems. Biblical justice is more than vindicating victims and punishing criminals. The intent of biblical justice is redemptive and attempts to restore the peace that existed before the offense.

PART AND PARCEL
Susie's Cries

"Today was my wedding day. Sam 'n' me stood in front of the chaplain and said our I do's. Mama brought a cake with lots of white icing and a bride and groom on top. The cake was the only part of my dream that came true.

"I used to dream about a happy wedding with flowers, candles, and me in a long, white dress. My family was together, and all my friends came to the party to eat the cake with lots of white icing.

"Tonight I lie in my bunk in a prison cell. I am lonely, angry. And I am remembering.

"The counselor asked me, 'Susie, what sights and sounds recur in your life?'

"That's easy to answer. All I see are tears and all I hear are cries.

"I hear my mama's fearful cry when Dad, in an alcoholic rage, throws her against the wall. I hear her sad cry trying to soothe her sick baby without medicine. I hear her muffled sobs at night knowing that we are hungry. I hear her lonely cry as Dad is sentenced to the county jail.

"I see dried tears on a scribbled note to him. 'Learn to read and write,' she screams at us.

"I see her timid tears as she opens the door to a group of women bringing a holiday charity package. I often wonder why she cries as she sorts the staples from the sweets.

"I hear my dad's cry of self-pity when he's gambled away his last cent. I hear his hostile cry at being indefinitely laid off the job. I hear his worried cry at realizing he will be labeled an ex-con.

"I hear the terrified cries of my brother and sister when the police arrest Dad. I hear their defensive sobs because of a classmate's ridicule, 'Dummies, why don't you wear shoes that fit?'

"I see my sister fling a textbook across the room with the painful cry, 'I can't see. My head hurts.'

"Through my own tears, I watched my family. To feed us, I stole. To relieve the boredom, I played 'hide-and-seek' with truant officers. To dull the daily problems, I injected drugs.

"The juvenile detention center became my home away from home.

"To be loved, I became pregnant with Sam's baby. To support myself, I sold drugs. Arrested in a drug bust, I'm serving my sentence in a prison 200 miles from my mama. I will give birth in the prison hospital. Until parole, Sam's aunt will raise our baby.

"The daily hurts of prison life would be unbearable without Mrs. Ray. Knowing that I was far from home, she asked to be my friend. Mrs. Ray listens to me. She understands about my baby. She began the legal procedure to permit our wedding. And she arranged for Sam and Mama to make the long trip today.

"I grew up in your town. My family still struggles there. My illiterate mama ekes out a meager living. My brother and sister roam your streets and play their own game of 'hide-and-seek' with truant officers. My dad wastes away in the county jail. My baby will be a new addition to your town.

"Can you hear our cries? Will you hear our cries?

"In prison, I have time to dream again. In my new dream, I am paroled and coming home. At the city limit sign, a nice lady, like Mrs. Ray, reaches out, saying, 'Welcome home, Susie. You can cry on my shoulder until all your tears are gone.'"

As ministers we desire to combat social and moral issues that ultimately lead people through the process of the criminal justice system. We desire to prevent people of all ages from becoming victims. We desire to extend justice for criminal behavior to reconciliation with family, the community, and God. As ministers we desire to ease the anxiety and uncertainty that characterize offenders' families. As ministers we desire to express appreciation to criminal justice employees and their families.

Parents and Children Together, Inc. (PACT), is a prison ministry in Fort Worth, Texas. A Hospitality House is one ministry among many PACT provides. Families of inmates are welcomed guests during their prison visits. The Moore family said, "It would not have been possible for the four of us to even come [for a visit] had it not been for the availability and conveniences of the Hospitality House."

PART AND PARCEL
Filling an Empty Nest Through Prison Ministry

"All I've ever wanted to be was a mom," says Sally Doster. "While raising my two sons, I had many wonderful experiences as a volunteer in schools, thrift store, legal aid offices, food banks, prisons, and nursing homes. After Ted left for college and Rob approached high school graduation, I prayed, really pleaded, with God to give me a ministry to fill my anticipated empty-nest loneliness. Through God's supernatural ways I was offered an opportunity to teach a parenting class at the US federal penitentiary. I was so excited that I had to seek God for two weeks before I could accept the offer. I was afraid that Sally, rather than God, had pushed open the door.

"Two days a week I have the blessing of presenting God's principles of life and parenting to men of many races, ages, backgrounds, and religions. We discuss repentance, forgiveness, self-sacrifice, and humility as well as communication techniques, choices and consequences, school involvement, and the art of listening. Discussions such as racism, finance, and priorities provide platforms for presenting God's truths and the need for prayer.

"The Lord has put His love for these men into my heart. These three years in my new 'mothering' role have brought me extraordinary joy and fulfillment. An added bonus is that my sons seem to enjoy sharing their mom, and my students are great listeners to stories about my boys.

"Please pray for my wisdom and boldness. Pray for the men I teach and for their families that their lives may be healed by Jehovah Rapha, the God Who heals.

"I pray for each of you to seek out the ministry God has prepared for you so that He can both use you and bless you."

PUZZLE PIECE
Imagine a Loving Home for All Children

Foster care is a ministry of reconciliation. Children need foster care for various reasons. Abuse and/or neglect result in children being removed from their homes.

Other times, because of illnesses or financial problems, parents are unable to provide for their children and require assistance until their situations change. Children from broken families need to be a part of a loving home.

Foster parents bless children by providing nutritious food, appropriate clothing, safe shelter, healthy exercise, and medical care. They give love, acceptance, a sense of self-worth, a set of values on which to make judgments, emotional control, and experiences of work and play. They offer an awareness of God's presence and an environment where children can learn to trust God.

PART AND PARCEL
Foster Parents

Foster parent Cindy Raley says, "I saw foster care as a ministry to reach out and give a child a second chance in life. In doing this, my reward has been the ability to adopt one of my foster children, enabling me to become a single parent. Now my daughter and I plan to continue our ministry by fostering other children," says foster parent Cindy Raley.

For foster parent Debby Grayson, "To reflect on foster parenting in a single statement is impossible for me because it has become a way of life. When my youngest of four children neared the end of his high school years, I prayed that God would direct my life in His service that would employ my increasing free time to His best purpose. He answered that prayer when my husband and I responded to a plea in our church bulletin for foster homes. We have been a part of the most enriching and personally gratifying ministry since then, and I have no doubt that we are squarely centered in the middle of God's will. You may ask how I am so certain.

"I can tell you that when you take in a battered, broken baby from the hospital at 5½ months, weighing only five pounds, who is blind and deaf from injury, whose dark skin is weathered and dry from dehydration, and whose faint cries are begging for love and devotion; and when you see this child, in the palm of God's healing hand, begin to grow gram by gram, day by day, into a laughing, squealing 18-month-old baby who can now see and hear, you have no doubt that you are responding to God's call."

Kandy Britnell feels that foster care fulfills Jesus' definition of ministry in Matthew 25:35–36. "Every time I am called about a child, our church immediately begins to pray for that child. Every child who comes into my home brings a renewing of love," she says.

"The greatest service I can offer is being a light on the path," says foster parent Gwendolyn May. "As long as I can remember, I have always wanted to help someone. In becoming a foster parent I have been able to do this in a very special way. Being a foster parent means you have to be a lighthouse for a child, to guide and protect them. You don't have to say much. Just let a child know that you are there should a need arise. Today I am devoted to shining the light of compassionate support and service on those who may be in need.

"I thank God for giving me the desire and commitment to helping to care for children."

PART AND PARCEL
Missionary for Internet Evangelism

Technology brings the world into our homes. Connecting with strangers who need the Lord opens many doors for ministry options. "Because of the Internet, the world is literally at our fingertips. With just a few keystrokes, we can shop, keep in touch with friends, and find out anything." North American Missionary Siam Rogers wants people to find Jesus Christ just as easily, and just as fast. As national missionary for Internet evangelism, Siam helps the North American Mission Board coordinate an evangelism presence on the Web. Besides hands-on Web site development, Siam also trains churches to use the Web as a tool to expand their ministries and share Christ.

Siam relates, "I was in a chat room one day having a conversation with a young lady in New Jersey. She was involved in every kind of ism there is: Mormonism, Hinduism, Buddhism. What began as a brisk and combative talk turned into four hours of dialogue. The Holy Spirit worked through that connection, and she prayed to receive Christ. She is now a seminary student."

Siam maintains a Web site at www.thegoodnews.org, which includes several gospel presentations. "After viewing the presentations, people can send an email indicating a profession of faith, desire to get involved in a local church, or ask questions. My greatest joy is to get those emails," says Siam.

Internet evangelism offers computer-savvy Christians another option to introduce lost people to Jesus.

MY PART
My Cluster Contains a Ministry Piece

If you had walked with Jesus in the first century, which of His physical needs would you have supplied? According the Jesus, the opportunity is still available: "Whatever you do for one of the least of these . . . you did for me" (Matt. 25:40).

Jesus described human need in personal terms: "For I was hungry and you gave me something to eat. I was thirsty and you gave me something to drink. I was a stranger and you invited me in. I needed clothes and you clothed me. I was sick and you looked after me. I was in prison and you came to visit me" (Matt. 25:35–36).

Which of these merciful acts can you accomplish alone? With others?

The unresolved struggles of Susie's family are multiplied many times in our communities. Examine each cry in Susie's story. How can your gift and resources of your Christian friends demonstrate:

• justice (advocating for social change or defending the unprotected)?

• mercy (identifying with another's pain)?

• a humble walk (becoming God's partner as He moves among hurting people)?

"I feel inadequate to minister," nonprofessional counselors frequently comment. We appreciate counselors who guide us through severe crises. However, the personal traits of empathy, warmth, and genuineness are basic ministering skills that develop as they are used.

Empathy is keeping your own objectivity intact while asking, "If I were she, how would I feel?"

Warmth is nonverbal caring—listening, sitting quietly, perhaps giving a hug, if appropriate.

Genuineness is a willingness to share yourself, being authentic. A cartoon shows an angry princess saying to the prince, "I like you better as a frog." When we allow our humanity to show, we are more winsome than when we try to appear flawless.

In a *Peanuts* comic strip, Charlie Brown describes the pitcher's mound as he faces the batter as "the loneliest place in the world."

"On the first pitch a line drive knocks Charlie Brown upside down and leaves him standing on his head.

"Running out to encourage Charlie Brown, Schroeder, his catcher, says, 'That first guy got a hit, Charlie Brown, but don't let it bother you. Just keep throwin' 'em in there!'

"'I'm upside down. I'm upside down,' responds Charlie Brown.

"Lucy walks in from the outfield. 'Hey, manager. Frieda's having a party after the game today. . . . She says you're welcome to come if you want to.'

"'I'm upside down. I'm upside down,' pleads Charlie Brown.

"No one notices Charlie Brown's predicament. His teammates act as though nothing has happened. . . .

"Snoopy, the Beagle shortstop, saves the day. He comes to the mound, takes off his cap, lays it on the ground, and stands on his head beside Charlie Brown. Then he gets up and goes back to his position."[1]

We "hear" each other on many occasions. We smile, shake hands, ask how things are going—not really wanting to know—but seldom notice when someone is upside down. We do not hear the feeling.

We can't "always turn a person right side up." At times "all we can do is take off our cap, stand on our head beside a person whose world is upside down, and let [her] know, 'I hear you. I care.'"[2]

Some puzzle pieces are connectors. They are vital to the puzzle but blend into the scenery. Jesus said to visit the prisons. We assume He meant offenders. But the criminal justice system employs many people such as judges, probation officers, wardens, guards, sheriffs, chaplains, and police. We can respond to Jesus' challenge and help relieve their stress by sending notes of appreciation, providing expense-paid dinners, and giving gift certificates to the employees and their families.

Some families are able to bring children into their homes. Others of us can assist in cooperative ministries. Pray over the ways you can assist foster parents:

- Adopt a foster family and support them emotionally, financially, and spiritually.
- Demonstrate to foster parents that you recognize and appreciate their ministry. Recognize them for what they are, missionaries in the home. A commissioning service before the entire church provides a blessing that foster parents never forget and can encourage them to rely on God and their church family when times become rough.
- Many foster parents have more than one child. Often they must herd several young children into church on Sunday mornings. Designate a parking spot or have people there to assist them.
- Assist families with foster children on birthdays. Bake or purchase a cake, and help in purchasing presents and/or decorations.
- Sponsor a foster child for Christmas.
- Sponsor a foster child as he or she prepares to go back to school with clothing and school supplies.
- Many foster children are behind their class in school; not because of their intellect, but because of the environment in which they have lived. Offer to tutor.
- Offer to baby-sit for free.
- When a new child comes into a home for the first time, treat the situation as you would a new baby. Offer to cook for the family. Help with clothing and toys.
- Make an effort to help a new child feel comfortable at your church. Prior to being placed in a Christian home, many foster children have never been inside a church. How your church chooses to accept or

reject the child will influence his view of Who God and Jesus are, who Christians are, and whether or not church is a safe place for them. A first impression is vital and a bad impression often takes years to overcome.

• Make a monetary gift to the Baptist children's home in your state.

Being a part of a team who has a heart for children helps you identify with Jesus' concern when He said, "Let the children come to me, and don't try to stop them! People who are like these children belong to God's kingdom" (Matt. 18:14 CEV).

In one community, friends gathered to pray for a family experiencing financial difficulties. As one person fervently prayed for God to bless the family, the pray-ers heard a loud knock on the door. The door opened to the son of a local farmer. Annoyed at the interruption of the prayer meeting, one person huffed, "What do you want?"

The boy replied, "Pa couldn't come, so I brought his prayers in the wagon! Come help me bring them in."

When the pray-ers saw the wagon, they learned that Pa's prayers consisted of potatoes, flour, beef, oatmeal, turnips, apples, jellies, and clothing.

God needs the praying heart with an open hand!

Now and then the ministry piece in my part of God's plan needs a tenderness overhaul.

"We can't sit in this pew. That girl has AIDS." And Ann, living with the HIV virus, exited in embarrassment.

"I didn't realize we had to teach the Bible through these bars. I'm not comfortable." And Cyndie, an inmate, felt rejected again.

"That child's family are troublemakers. Let's move to other swings." And Marlo, who is eight, wondered why no one shared the seesaw or slide.

Step meditatively into Mark 1:40–42. Warning of his presence, a pathetic dreg of humanity approaches. Recoiling with mixed feelings of pity and terror, we cross the street wondering how one of them could be in our neighborhood. After all, lepers in our town are shunned as untouchables and banished from society to live in their own section. Why bother with lepers? They are dead men walking.

Then Jesus steps into our meditation and into the scene. Viewing from a safe distance, we see the leper kneel at Jesus' feet and plaintively weep. Surely Jesus, Who is antiseptically clean as we are, will shrink back. But with compassion, not contempt, Jesus' hands touch the loathsome leper with instantaneous healing. His love and power are commensurate.

Life situations change. Society is precarious. The possibility is that one day we could be them.

Father, push us to follow Jesus' example of seeing, reaching out, and touching.

[1]John Hendrix, ed., *On Becoming a Group* (Nashville: Broadman Press, n.d.), 42.
[2]Ibid., 42–43.

7

GOD'S PLAN *To Keep Us*
MY PART *To Trust His Care*

"So do not be ashamed to testify about our Lord, or ashamed of me his prisoner. But join with me in suffering for the gospel, by the power of God, who has saved us and called us to a holy life—not because of anything we have done but because of his own purpose and grace. This grace was given us in Christ Jesus from the beginning of time" (2 Tim. 1:8–9).

We sat at the table shuffling the puzzle pieces. A national disaster preempted enjoyment of assembling the puzzle, "Tempting Sweets." In fact, the leisure to work a puzzle seemed inappropriate.

Our conversation centered on a columnist's comment that each era contained "turbulent years that brought global depression, genocide, war, political assassination, social upheaval, and the specter of revolution."

Religious freedom is at risk in many countries. Human rights abuses are prevalent around the globe. Violence and discrimination against religious minorities persist. Perpetrators of the atrocities are not brought to justice.

Working the puzzle was the antithesis of suffering, and like my life, rarely inconvenienced to the point of crisis; never persecuted for righteousness.

By the way, when was your most recent experience in being persecuted for Jesus' sake?

PUZZLE PIECE
Imagine Paul Alone in Prison

Paul's second imprisonment was different from his first. He was jailed first as a political prisoner, awaiting trial. Now he is a condemned criminal, awaiting death. His arrest may have been sudden, explaining why he left without taking his coat and scrolls (2 Tim. 4:13).

During his first detention, he lived in his own house. Now he huddles in a dungeon.

Many friends visited during his first imprisonment. Now he is deserted.

Paul urged Timothy to be unashamed of him, a prisoner, and of the gospel they both preached: God loves us, sent His Son to die for us, raised Him from the dead, gave us eternal life, and calls us to a holy life.

Epaphroditus was an example to Timothy on how to live with danger. He did not let a menacing society threaten his friendship with Paul but instead traveled to Rome to minister to Paul in prison. In those days when people visited prisoners, they were labeled criminal types. A prison visitor risked being exposed to peril just by being near prisoners.

In addition to bringing physical and emotional encouragement to Paul, Epaphroditus brought money from the Philippian believers. Paul referred to Epaphroditus as "brother . . . fellow worker . . . fellow soldier . . . messenger . . . minister to my need" (Phil 2:25 RSV).

Epaphroditus never asked, "How great is the risk?" He asked, "When do you need me?"

Risks, trials, and humiliations are opportunities for Christ to demonstrate His power in us. Courageous suffering is possible because the power that saved us will sustain us. Suppose the problem is lack of desire to obey when faced with dangerous situations. Take to heart Philippians 2:13: "For it is God who works in you to will and to act according to his good purpose." Ask God to motivate your weak will, your want-to attitude.

Paul's request for Timothy "to take your share of suffering" is an indictment to a comfortable lifestyle that insulates us from standing with Jesus in society. Not suffering means we have limited life to a series of church meetings with like-minded friends. We have isolated ourselves from people who desperately need Jesus. We protect a satisfactory faith that saves from hell but fails to have an impact on our routine. Paul was a prisoner for the gospel's sake. Although the gospel is a message of peace, it brings a sword wherever preached (Matt. 10:34–39).

Paul's request for Timothy to share the suffering is an indictment to how well we cultivate Christ's qualities. When we live Christ's attitudes and behavior, we will be broadsided by the world's ways. When we are humble, the proud call us simpletons. When we are yoked to God, the powerful call us weak. When we are sensitive, the tough call us do-gooders. When we are righteous in word and deed, the skeptics call us prudes.

The responses of an unsaved society to God's message of grace are disgust, contrived put-downs, snubs, discrimination, insults, and laughter. When we live Jesus' disposition, persecution is inevitable. More than a casual observer, Jesus shares our suffering and offers hope. "In this world you will have trouble. But take heart! I have overcome the world" (John 16:33).

Paul's request for Timothy to join in the suffering causes us to examine the true meaning of persecution. Jesus did not congratulate Christians who are opposed because of our own negligence, meddling, or rudeness. He did not congratulate those who experience hardships or heartaches by harboring regrets, guilt, or remorse. Jesus affirmed believers who are persecuted for living right.

The Pharisees hated Jesus because His holiness made their righteousness seem like rags. Living the Beatitudes (Matt. 5:3–12), Christians become a threat to society's status quo. Daring to be different from society's standards, Christians suffer oppression and harassment for Jesus' sake. Paul reminded Timothy, "In fact, everyone who wants to live a godly life in Christ Jesus will be persecuted" (2 Tim. 3:12).

Jesus told His followers to rejoice when persecuted because of loyalty to Him. Persecution forces us to rethink priorities, points out superficial beliefs, strengthens the importance of Christ in our lives, and proves our faithfulness. "Dear friends, do not be surprised at the painful trial you are suffering, as though something strange were happening to you. But rejoice that you participate in the sufferings of Christ, so that you may be overjoyed when His glory is revealed. If you are insulted because of the name of Christ, you are blessed, for the Spirit of glory and God rests on you. . . . If you suffer as a Christian, do not be ashamed, but praise God that you bear that name" (1 Peter 4:12–14,16).

As Jesus' partners in suffering, we will receive His grace (2 Tim. 1:8–9); share His work and experience His power (Phil. 3:10); receive His comfort and ability to empathize with others (2 Cor. 1:7); extend the church (Col. 1:24); share His glory (1 Peter 5:1); follow His example (1 Peter 2:19); receive His mercy (James 5:10–11); and gain God's perspective (1 Peter 5:10). "Rejoice and be glad, because great is your reward in heaven" (Matt. 5:12).

Paul recognized that God would meet his needs (Phil. 4:11). Yet his sufferings recorded in 2 Corinthians 11:23–27 astound us. Paul saw opportunities in difficulties. To the Corinthians, he wrote, "But I will stay on at Ephesus until Pentecost, because a great door for effective work has opened to me, and there are many who oppose me" (1 Cor. 16:8–9). The conjunction *and* is the key word in this statement. We might be tempted to write *but* instead of *and*, as if adversaries would make the opportunities impossible. Paul wrote *and* as if to say so what? He did not allow difficulties to negate the opportunity.

Paul lived in a violent, terroristic society. In the first century, Jewish zealots resisted Roman rule through violent assassinations. Attackers called knifewielders blended into the crowds at festivals. Surrounded by sympathizers, they murdered soldiers and disappeared into the crowds. In retribution, the Roman government suppressed their opponents with state-sponsored terrorism.

Paul responded to terrorism in ways we can emulate. For safety reasons, he worked within the legal system (Acts 23:17). He avoided violence (Acts 17:10; 19:8–9,30–31). He used the attacks and trials as opportunities to preach the gospel (Acts 26).

Paul remained in the Roman dungeon facing his hour of execution triumphantly. "I have fought the good fight. I have finished the race, I have kept the faith. Now there is in store for me the crown of righteousness, which the Lord, the righteous Judge, will award to me on that day—and not only to me, but also to all who have longed for His appearing" (2 Tim. 4:7–8).

Nothing happens to us apart from God's permission. God permitted the alliance of Herod, Pilate, the Gentiles, and unbelieving Jews to be the perpetrators of His will for Jesus to suffer unjustly (Acts 2:23; 4:28–29).

Recognition of God's sovereignty must saturate my part in God's plan.

Jesus promised trouble in this life. In the same breath, He promised peace (John 16:33), an inner calm that shines brighter during the crisis than in the resolution.

PUZZLE PIECE
Imagine a Question Mark

"But he knows the way I take" (Job 23:10). At times I'm tempted to read Job's statement as a question: Does God really know the way I take?

When my part includes suffering, I'm tempted to ask why. The essential point is the attitude of the question, not the question itself.

Why is not flung from a fist raised in rage at an impersonal power.

Why is not spoken to a whimsical god who delights in a game of "eeny meany miney mo, now it is your time to go."

Why is not a sigh of stoical resignation.

Why is not asked to satisfy a logical mind.

Why is not asked in the spirit of wounded pride.

Many experiences are punctuated with whys. You know about them. They are times when you and God are partners in a mystery, times when the communication is so tender that you and God share in the silence of why.

The whys formed in the depths of sincere feelings, agonizing emotions, and questioning minds honor God. Questioning is more an act of faith than is silent submission. Implicit in the asking is the faith that an answer exists. Our insistent why finds its sufficient answer in the comforting words of Job, "He knows!" (Job 23:10).

PUZZLE PIECE
Imagine Blood-Stained Continents on the Globe

Job said, "But he knows the way I take." God knows about a Chinese church leader who, over a period of years, has been beaten and imprisoned for his faith. In response to how Christians could pray for the church in China, he asked not for prayer for the release of imprisoned Christians or for an end to persecution. "Pray instead that those who are suffering will sense God's presence with them and that He will be glorified through their lives and witness."

God knows that six men broke into the home of Gaiton Zimulinda, pastor of a church in West Africa. His wife and children watched as the attackers murdered Zimulinda and drew a cross on the wall with his blood.

God knows that in an Asian labor camp, Christians were beaten, sexually abused, starved, tortured, and even killed in efforts to force them to recant their faith.

God knows that a guard in an iron-smelting factory tried to force eight Christians to deny their faith. When they refused, the guard had molten iron poured over them. The metal shriveled their bodies into nothing.

God knows that Ayub Masih was convicted on false charges of blasphemy against the state religion. In solitary confinement, he suffers deplorable conditions: no light, no toilet facility, no fan in a cell where temperatures reach 120°F.

God knows that in Benin a young believer and her three children have been rejected by her fetisher husband, who recently had taken a third wife. Saying she spends too much time at church and does not obey him, he stopped supporting her in any way. She goes from field to field, working for neighbors and earning only a few coins or some produce in return. Yet Christian workers say she has remained in her home—showing respect and kindness to her husband—and faithfully continues to serve in her church.

God knows that 440 million children in China do not know Christ. Teaching children about Christ is risky because the government prohibits anyone under the age of 18 from being baptized or becoming a church member. Nevertheless, a number of churches in China reach out to children with Bible classes and activities that will allow them to know of Christ's love.

God knows that 3 children of a pastor in Asia—aged 5, 7, and 8—attended a school in which students were required to memorize Buddhist Scriptures and recite them in class. The youngest child refused because she knew her family believed in Jesus Christ. Her teacher beat her for refusing. After praying about what to do, the children began reciting Bible verses and singing Christian songs. The youngest child's teacher stopped beating her, and the older children's teacher began visiting their home to talk to their father about Jesus.

God knows that house churches have been growing rapidly among Hmong minorities in a Southeast Asia country. The government responded by jamming gospel radio broadcasts into the country. Several Hmong Christian leaders are in prison because of their evangelistic activities.

God knows about women who live in fear and ignorance. Lack of education seriously hampers the lives of women in many parts of the world, often in unexpected ways. A Christian worker in East Asia told a woman about Christ and invited her to a Christian gathering. She was shocked when the woman told her she would not attend because she did not know how to ride the elevator that would take her to the meeting place on a building's upper floor.

God knows about the death and rape threats against believers in Sri Lanka if they continue to hold worship services. Masked men smashed the church property in the early morning hours. The pastor was leading a prayer meeting when the mob, wielding machetes, terrorized the congregation.

MY PART
My Cluster Contains Prayer for the Persecuted Church

The gnu, a large African antelope, has an interesting, instructive habit. When it meets an enemy, it quickly kneels and springs to attack from its knees.

From your knees, grapple with needs of the persecuted church. Cry out to God:
- to comfort believers who suffer for the name of Jesus Christ;
- to execute justice on behalf of imprisoned believers;
- to give His peace to believers enduring tribulations;
- to give believers boldness to witness;
- to multiply the number of believers in places of persecution;
- to convict the hearts of persecutors and turn them to Christ;
- to frustrate government attempts that hinder the preaching of the gospel;
- to raise up a great number of Spirit-filled leaders;
- to protect gospel radio broadcasts and to draw seekers to listen
- to direct follow-up efforts from radio broadcasts and showings of the *Jesus* film;
- to speed the production of Christian literature for every people group;
- to protect Christians who live in restrictive and dangerous places;

- to turn Satan's evil schemes to good;
- to bind evil spirits who inspire violence;
- to give boldness to workers who lead children;
- to protect Christians who risk their lives taking the Bible into hostile places;
- to put a hunger for the truth in the hearts of leaders of other religions;
- to break down barriers of secularism and materialism that hinder Europeans from receiving the gospel;
- to empower all of us to pray visionary prayers.

Father, as Your heart breaks for lost people, give us that same heartache.

From your knees, rejoice in answered prayer for the persecuted.

- A missionary family in Haiti had been without telephone service for many months. One day a telephone repairman unexpectedly appeared at their door to repair their phone. Soon after the repair, their first call came from a young woman who had recently become a believer and needed help sharing Christ with her family. Not only did God, in His providence, send a long-overdue repairman at just the right time, but the missionary family had no idea where the young woman even got their phone number. God reigns even over telephone companies.
- An Indian priest in the temple of Kali, Hindu goddess of destruction, watched the *Jesus* film. Deeply moved at Jesus' sacrifice of His own life, the priest gave his heart to Christ. As he shared the good news of deliverance from sin, 86 people in his village gave their hearts to Jesus. Thank the Lord for delivering the priest from the pagan goddess.
- Ninety people in a large Chinese city accepted Christ after meeting believers in an English-teaching

program. Several new groups were begun as a result. One believer said, "Our biggest problem was that we didn't believe this could happen!" Thank God for these new believers. Ask Him to preserve them in their faith.

- Two missionaries risked imprisonment to take 300 Bibles into a country where the government was hostile to Christian witness. After delivering their cargo, the workers realized they faced a new problem. On the way in, their van had cleared a low tunnel only because it was weighted down with the Bibles. Now it would be too tall to enter the tunnel. At a checkpoint, policemen ordered the pair to give a ride to four very large soldiers. The van sank enough under the soldiers' weight to clear the tunnel. The missionaries were able to return the van home to use for a future trip. Thank God for believers who take risks to carry God's Word into hostile places.

- When a worker in China prayed last fall that she would see 300 students on her university campus come to Christ during the school year, friends shook their heads and laughed at the unrealistic goal. But God heard and honored her prayer. At year's end, more than 300 students had accepted the Lord as Savior. Glorify God for honoring her visionary prayer.

- Christians planning to start a church in Papenburg, Germany, asked God help them find a place to meet. A well-known businessman called a team member and said he had had a dream and wanted to provide a room in a prime location for their meetings. The church would pay only the heating costs. The businessman, who was not a Christian, provided money for the building's renovation. Rejoice in the Lord over the way He provides for His people when they are obedient to His will.

- Many people in western Guatemala think that all missionaries have a gold mine in the mountains. Why else would an international come to such an isolated and forsaken spot? When a national accepted Jesus as Savior, a friend asked him if he now also had a gold mine. "I have something far more valuable than a gold mine," the new believer replied. "I have the Word of God." The new believer is now translating the Bible into the language of his people so they will hear the message more valuable than gold. Praise God for spreading His word.

- Believers prayed for a congregation in Guatemala that was driven out of town by hostile citizens who then burned the church building. When a missionary recently returned to the town, he found 75 people waiting—one of them a man who had helped burn the church building. Over 2 years, he had been touched by the way other believers had come to encourage the local believers and the way God had protected His church. Glorify God for using the persecution of His people to be a witness to His life-changing power.

- An older ethnic Korean woman went from China to South Korea to look for relatives. It was her first time to be in Korea. Since she had no place to stay, she slept in a mission church. During her stay, she saw the *Jesus* film in Chinese and studied the Scriptures several times with local believers. She became a believer. Before leaving, she said, "I came to find my relatives and did not find any. But I found Someone more important—Jesus." Praise God for giving the Korean woman the most precious gift of all. Praise Him for sending a witness back into her Chinese village.

- A team of Mongolian believers braved strong winds and heavy snow to share the gospel in remote areas of their country. Yet God was faithful to draw people to Christ throughout the 3,000-mile trip. When the battery in their vehicle froze in a mining town, a small group of men stopped to help. By the time the truck started, three of the men had accepted Christ. In another village, a family of four accepted Christ. In another village, an elderly couple became Christians and were baptized. And in the next village, eight teenaged boys were baptized. Thank God for opening the hearts of these people to the truth of the gospel.

- A businessman in Albania was seriously wounded when someone attacked him with a knife. As his Christian neighbors prayed for him at the hospital, he became convinced God had protected him from death. Soon after, the man publicly declared his faith in Christ during his youngest son's wedding. The whole family accepted Christ. The local television station, which recorded the entire event on tape, showed the scene every day for the next week. Now a house church meets in the newlywed couple's home. Thank God for using a crisis to reveal Himself to this man and his family.

- In Romania, Christian crisis pregnancy clinics are making a difference in the lives of women. Christian counselors share the gospel of God's love. Over 200 women have received Christ as Savior. Praise God for counselors who care for the body and the soul.

- A young woman in Spain met a group of young Christians who were witnessing on the streets of her city. She was amazed at the joy and peace they demonstrated. When she returned to talk to the team, they were gone. As she walked away, she noticed a gospel tract on the sidewalk where someone had thrown it. Then she saw another and another. She followed the trail of discarded tracts to the place where the team was singing and witnessing. After she had given her heart to Christ, she wrote, "Dear God, thank You for those gospel booklets. The printed page saved my life!"

- A young believer in Niger accidentally left behind a gospel audiotape while visiting some friends. When the friends realized the contents of the tape, they tried to erase it. When one attempt failed, they tried another cassette player, again unsuccessfully. The whole group became afraid and one young man, the son of a high-ranking religious leader, went to the believer and gave his heart to Jesus Christ. Praise God for small displays of His power that show He is in control and can draw all people to Himself.

- God unexpectedly led a believer to a Mongolian Christian who was excited about starting churches in districts of a large city where people live in the traditional round Mongolian tents. The two left for one of the districts, looking for anyone interested in a church. In one tent, they discovered a family of believers who had desired to start a church in that district for some time. They had built an extra-large house a year earlier in hopes of using it as a gathering place for believers. Thank God for miraculously leading His children to each other. Thank Him for speaking to the family and preparing them for the arrival of this church planting team.

- After hearing God's Word through Bible storying sessions, people in several villages in East Africa wanted to read it for themselves. None of them could read and they did not have a teacher. They sent a delegation of men to a missionary teacher's home. Since none of the men had a vehicle, they walked through the hot sand, hitched a ride on a donkey cart, or paid a few precious coins to travel the distance. As a result of their trip, a two-week literacy workshop was held to train someone from each of the villages. Thank God for the sincere desire for God's Word these men demonstrated. Praise God for literacy training.

- In Senegal, a group listened attentively to the Genesis 22 account of the testing of Abraham. One astute listener wanted to talk about the sacrifice (a ram) that God provided. The group discussed how each year they and their families sacrifice a ram at a solemn occasion when they remember the day Abraham was ordered to sacrifice his son. They noted that these rams are expensive and purchased by the head of the household. But for Abraham, God provided the sacrifice. Praise God for teaching His truth.

- In China, Christian organizations are working hard to develop gospel materials that can be effectively shared electronically. Thank God for information technology.

- A year after the TransWorld Radio commissioned a new transmitter to broadcast the gospel in India, more than 1 million letters flooded their offices. People wanted to know more about Jesus. More than 60 churches were established in the country. Praise God for gospel radio broadcasters who take the message of His love to people waiting to hear.

- Customs officials seized a small load of New Testaments being carried into a Last Frontier country that is openly hostile to the gospel of salvation in Jesus Christ. When a Christian worker went to try to claim them a few days later, the customs officials were very open and pleasant toward him. They told the worker they could not return the New Testament, but asked, "Do you mind if each one of our workers takes one of the Holy Books with him?" Thank God that His ways are above our ways. Praise Him for seeds that were planted in the hearts of these officials.

- An Uzbekistan government official publicly hailed the Bible as "a priceless source of knowledge." His remarks came during a ceremony marking the first local publication of an Uzbek edition of Proverbs, the first book of the Bible ever published in the Uzbek language. Praise God for bypassing the legal restrictions on importing Christian literature into the country.
- A Christian woman in an African people group hurried the missionary along muddy, slippery paths to visit neighbors she had prayed for and witnessed to. As time grew short, the woman moved faster and faster. As they came to each house, the missionary shared a Bible story and every family member prayed to receive Christ. And each time, the woman would hurry off again, calling over her shoulder, "These people are very lost."

The persevering witness of oppressed believers awakens our heartfelt desire for each persecuted person to experience Psalm 4:8. "I will lie down and sleep in peace, for you alone, O Lord, make me dwell in safety."

The African woman's urgency to tell about Jesus burdens us to keep our feet on the path to our lost neighbors.

Consider the witnessing experiences of persecuted Christians. Do we dare ask, "Do our lives now or in the future contain a piece labeled *martyr?*"

When we see the word *witness,* the shadow word is *martyr.*

When we hear the word *witness,* the echo cries *martyr.*

Being an unashamed witness is an attitude and a purpose for living, not a plan.

Jesus promised great rewards to those who suffer for His sake (Matt. 5:10–12). Our prayer is, "Lord, make me righteous enough to deserve persecution for it."

8

GOD'S PLAN   *To Hear*
MY PART   *To Pray*

"I want everyone everywhere to lift innocent hands toward heaven and pray" (1 Tim. 2:8 CEV).

Deep in thought, we sat at the puzzle table enjoying each other's company and occasionally fitting a piece into the "Tempting Sweets" puzzle. Someone mentioned seeing a puzzle glued together as a permanent picture. We reminisced about past scenes from favorite puzzles. I mentioned Michelangelo's painting *The Creation of Adam* as my favorite. In fact, I had seen the actual painting in the Sistine Chapel.

Michelangelo painted an image of God reaching out to the sleeping Adam to give him the spark of life. God's arm is strong. His finger, pointing accurately toward Adam's hand, is sure of its purpose. In contrast, Adam's listless fingers curve instead of reaching toward his Creator. The fingers do not touch. A slight space separates them.

Prayer is like that space between God's fingers, constantly, consistently, untiringly stretched toward my own weak, busy, bent ones. I wish our fingers constantly touched. They don't. I seek ways to improve our communication. The search is worth the struggle. When our fingers touch, I feel penetrating power, perceptive poise, and a precious peace.

Prayer is the adhesive that keeps the pieces of life's cluster focused on doing my part in God's plan.

PUZZLE PIECE
Imagine Hands Lifted in Praise

Praise is one element of prayer that helps us stay close to God. Though beautiful, our English language is limited. We use praise to encompass all kinds of grateful expressions. However, the Scriptures have specific words for praise. Consider three of them.

Hallelu is one word for praise. Hallelu is glorifying and adoring God just for being God. Hallelu is praising God for His intangible qualities residing within us, like power, love, and self-control.

Peace is an intangible quality of God that Paul mentions in the salutations of all his letters. Perhaps peace, with the exception of grace, soothed Paul more than any other of the Lord's characteristics. Peace was a catalyst in Paul's chaotic world.

Baracha is another Hebrew word for praise. Baracha involves praising God for His tangible favors and benefits: people, places, possessions, and pleasures.

Reading Acts and Paul's letters without interruption helped me see Paul, the man. He was grateful for the homes of Lydia, Titus Justus, Jason, Mnason (Acts 21:16), and Priscilla and Aquila. He missed his books. He was thankful for his tentmaking skill. He appreciated the monetary gifts.

Baracha praises God for all we experience through our senses: tasting chocolate or popcorn, smelling a rose or coffee perking, seeing a sunset or home, hearing waves lap the shore or footsteps of the children.

As I drove to the retreat, the odometer on my car turned over to 98,000 miles. Glancing at the zeroes clicking over, my thoughts expressed concern about the mechanics of the vehicle. Perhaps the mileage is a message to participate in ministries requiring less travel by automobile, I thought.

Returning home from the retreat, I saw in the driveway a sports car pitted with hail indentions. This is the story: Not long after I left for the retreat, my husband learned that a car dealership was selling hail-damaged cars for half price. He bought one—a brand-new, pockmarked car with 0 miles.

The Lord has a sense of humor. The lean and lanky, whistling and swaggering young man carted my groceries through the parking lot. He steered me toward a sleek sedan. Was he amazed when I passed the sedan and flipped open the hatchback of the sports car!

"This ya vehicle?" he drawled.

"Sure is."

"Right on, Mama!" he exclaimed with gusto.

Other more serious times when people at the gas pumps ask about the hail indentions, I share how the Lord helped our budget. The little car is a possession eliciting baracha praise.

Hymnos is a Greek praise word. The experience of Paul and Silas in the Philippian prison describes the attitude of hymnos. "At midnight Paul and Silas were praying and singing hymns to God" (Acts 16:25).

Hymnos is not a stoic pretense that the circumstance is good. Hymnos praise recognizes God's all-sufficient strength in crises. It lifts our soul above the circumstances to the reality that God is in control.

When we share our difficulties with the Lord, He helps us see them from His perspective. The caterpillar, as it creeps along the ground, has a very different view of the world from what it will have when wings develop. As a butterfly, it will soar above the places where it once crawled. The problem that seems like an impassable wall becomes an insignificant line when viewed from above.

God does not always choose to give us answers here. However, how does this statement affect my part in God's plan? "We are receiving exactly what we would request if we could see as God sees!"

PUZZLE PIECE
Imagine a Figure Lying Prostrate

Confession cleanses us to do our part. Paul quoted David's acknowledgement of God's forgiveness: "God blesses people whose sins are forgiven and whose evil deeds are forgotten. The Lord blesses people whose sins are erased from his book" (Rom. 4:7–8 CEV).

In Psalm 51, David struggled with a personal agony. Nathan, the prophet, had confronted David with his sins of murder and adultery (2 Sam. 12:1–9). Realizing his condition before God, David sobbed his confession. A mighty military commander stood defenseless. A wealthy king possessed nothing to qualify him to come before God.

Meditate on Psalm 51 and listen as David cast himself on God's mercy. David's image pales into the background as your image emerges, crying out to God: "Lord, I'm to blame for my sin, not the genes I inherited, not society's standards.

"I have committed treason against the King of kings. Please, Lord, erase the record of my rebellion. Scrub me repeatedly until the last stain disappears. Purify my corrupt heart. Refresh my spirit. Restore my joy.

"Lord, with a willing spirit, I will do my part. I will teach Your ways and sing Your righteousness to sinners who will turn to You. Amen."

PUZZLE PIECE
Imagine a Figure Kneeling

Join Daniel in this petition prayer: "Now, our God, hear the prayers and petitions of your servant" (Dan. 9:17).

Petitions are the important "me" prayers: help, guide, hear, give, and teach. Add your favorite "me" prayers. Petition prayers enable us to cultivate the fruit of the Spirit as we ask to be more like Jesus. God never says no to your persistent request to be more like Jesus. When our faith is victorious over life's difficulties, we rush into God's presence with praise for His help. When doubts cause us to flounder and fail, our cries petition God for His help.

In petition praying, does the real you kneel before God? Or does a dramatist perform words you think God wants to hear? In Matthew 6:5–8, Jesus teaches the importance of private communion. "When you pray, go into your room, close the door, and pray to your Father, Who is unseen. Then your Father, Who sees what is done in secret, will reward you" (v. 6).

PART AND PARCEL
Prayer Altars

The siblings often smiled at their 90-year-old mother's comment, "No need to plan a funeral when I die. I've outlived all my friends." When their mother died, the children were pleasantly surprised to see the church filled with mourners of all ages and from every strata of the city's society. Grieving, they offered condolences, celebrated the life, and commemorated the "passage through the portals," their friend's poetic reference to death.

Sometime after the funeral, the children gathered at the stately Victorian house on the corner in the old neighborhood. As they cleared away personal items, they mentioned the unusual attendance at the funeral.

In a semifinished attic space off their mother's bedroom, they discovered the reason. A rocking chair pulled close to the dormer window had worn indentions in the floor from hours of gentle rocking. A neatly folded shawl rested over the chair's arm. Impressions of kneeling knees had worn through the tapestry covering of the footstool.

Piled around the chair were Bibles and other inspirational material. In an open journal were names of people, their needs, and dates of answered prayer. Thank-you notes, expressing gratitude for their mother's prayers, spilled from a box.

The children recognized that many of the names in the journals and notes were of people they had met at the service.

Their mother's altar was an attic space with a Bible, a rocking chair, and a footstool.

She is a young pastor's wife, the mother of three active sons. Her busy lifestyle is exciting. Yet without personal attention to her own relationship with God, the activities will extinguish her spiritual and emotional energy.

She has an altar, a place dedicated to commune with God. Her literal closet is under the stairs off the foyer. The space is just the right size for a stool, a small table holding her Bible, family pictures, and devotional material. A tiny space to scoot into for a moment's respite soothes and renews her spirit.

PUZZLE PIECE
Imagine a Kneeling Figure Holding a Globe

Intercession is asking God to work in the life of someone else. It involves the Trinity because we present desires in the name of God the Son, initiated in the mind by God the Holy Spirit, and trust God the Father to answer.

Paul's letters reveal some interesting prayer concepts, including one found in 2 Corinthians 1:11: "As you help us by your prayers, then many will give thanks on our behalf for the gracious favor granted us in answer to the prayers of many."

Paul was in Philippi when he wrote the second letter to the Corinthians. He asked the Christians to cooperate with him in his work by their prayers. "As you help us by your prayers" means "working together underneath." Prayer is a tunnel through which the gospel power runs. As an intercessor, tunnel your prayers into every nation, every neighborhood of your city, and every opponent of the gospel. Watch the astonishment when the power erupts!

Another fascinating concept is that intercessors are wrestlers. "Epaphras, who is one of you and a servant of Christ Jesus, sends greetings. He is always wrestling in prayer for you, that you may stand firm in all the will of God, mature, and fully assured" (Col. 4:12).

Epaphras interceded with deep love and concern for the believers in his church family. Paul explained how Epaphras expended time and strength in intercession as he was always in prayer. Epaphras prayed with the same agonizing exertions as a wrestler struggles with an opponent.

Like Epaphras, we should be prayer wrestlers and rise from our knees exhausted.

As we intercede for others, a humbling reality is that Christ intercedes for us (Heb. 7:25; Rom. 8:34).

When you recall with awe how God's mercy through Jesus' blood covers your sins, remember Christ interceded for your lostness (Isa. 53:12).

When your soul rhapsodizes with extravagant enthusiasm because through Jesus' behavior and words you know God, remember Jesus prays for believers (John 17:6–9).

When you experience remarkable answers to prayer, superhuman strength, unexplainable events, and timely defense from danger, remember Christ intercedes for your protection (John 17:11).

When you feel self-controlled and alert, although you realize Satan is causing you to doubt your relationship with God, remember Jesus prays for your security through God's powerful name (Luke 22:32; John 17:11–12).

When you exult in joy for escaping the corruption surrounding you, remember Christ intercedes for your purity (John 17:17).

When you experience forgiveness by confessing sins, remember your Advocate stands in your place before God (1 John 2:1–2).

When you meet a human you once categorized and see a person not a label, remember Jesus prays for our unity (John 17:21–23).

How amazing! We are the answers to Christ's prayers.

PUZZLE PIECE
Imagine the Heavenly Throne

"Let us then approach the throne of grace with confidence, so that we may receive mercy and find grace to help us in our time of need" (Heb. 4:16).

The destination of our prayers is the throne of grace. Often we leap with praise toward the throne. Now and then, we limp along shackled with unconfessed sin. Other times we lag behind embarrassed by inconsistent intercession and apathetic petitions. But true prayer is the approach to the throne regardless of feelings that cause us to leap, limp, or lag behind. Prayer is the want-to of our souls to come near to God even before we think about voicing praises or needs.

Our approach is one of

• reverence toward our Creator in a familial parent-child relationship. When Jesus modeled a prayer for us, He called God, Our Father (or Abba), the affectionate Hebrew name meaning daddy. He gave us a new dimension of intimacy. *Abba* is a soft word. Repeat it several times. Notice that you did not form Abba by using your teeth. Abba is a sensitive, profound sigh between the lips.

Jesus qualified our calling God, Abba by describing God's infinite greatness: "Who art in heaven" and His royalty, "hallowed be thy name." Reverent familiarity is appropriate. Boldness is invited. Impertinence is taboo.

• submission by requesting in every prayer the reservation, "Thy will be done."

• expectation by recognizing that God's ways and thoughts are far above our own and by asking God to do exceeding abundantly above what we ask or think.

• confidence before One Who forgives sins and helps in time of need.

PUZZLE PIECE
Imagine a Threshold Sprinkled with Blood

The threshold to the throne of grace is the sacrifice of Christ. "Therefore . . . since we have confidence to enter the Most Holy Place by the blood of Jesus, by a new and living way opened for us through the curtain, that is, his body and since we have a great priest over the house of

126

God, let us draw near to God with a sincere heart in full assurance of faith, having our hearts sprinkled to cleanse us from a guilty conscience" (Heb. 10:19–22).

In Old Testament days, a veil barred access into the Holy of Holies, the place of prayer in the tabernacle and temple. One day each year the High Priest pulled aside the veil and entered with the blood sacrifice he offered to God. When Christ died, His blood became our sacrifice: His broken body, tearing the veil, became our threshold into the throne of grace. Christ offered a new way of conveying the idea of newly slain. His one sacrifice remains as fresh as if He died yesterday; as if His blood was shed for us this morning.

Does Calvary have a date? The Lamb was slain before the foundation of the world (Rev. 13:8; 1 Peter 1:19–20) and will be recognized through eternity as "a Lamb . . . as if it had been slain" (Rev. 5:6). As you pass through the threshold of Christ's precious blood into the throne of grace, be overwhelmed with His love.

PART AND PARCEL
Paul Just Prayed

My conclusion to a search of Paul's letters for a commentary on prayer became, "He just prayed." He just prayed. Paul did not list reasons for praying or explain the benefits of prayer or describe a form to follow. He just prayed assuming that prayer was a normal expression for believers.

Paul formed prayers with definite purposes. For example, 2 Corinthians 12:1–10 is a prayer for deliverance and how God will work through our weaknesses; while Ephesians 3:14–21 is a prayer for inner growth. For Paul prayer was unceasing (2 Tim. 1:3) in the sense of recurring again and again. Intercession for others and their needs was an essential part of his spiritual experience. The prayers for the churches and the believers reveal matters he thought were important for their growth (Col. 2:1–3).

Paul's prayers were vigorous. He used strong illustrations like a laborer working with all his energy (Col. 1:29), an athlete contending for the coveted prize (1 Cor. 9:25), a soldier fighting for his life (1 Tim. 6:12).

Paul also asked others to pray for him. In 2 Corinthians 1:8–11, he linked success of his work to the prayer support of Christians. To Paul, prayer was a cooperative effort among believers. He asked prayer for boldness in speaking (Acts 4:29), open doors to witness (Col. 4:3), deliverance (Gal. 1:4), protection from unreasonable or dangerous people (2 Thess. 3:2), and people to receive his ministry (Rom. 15:31).

Paul prayed with confidence. Prayer was appropriate in every circumstance. He expected God's intervention.

PUZZLE PIECE
Imagine a Dove and Praying Hands

At the throne of grace, the Holy Spirit intercedes for us. "We do not know what we ought to pray for, but the Spirit himself intercedes for us with groans that words cannot express. And he who searches our hearts knows the mind of the Spirit, because the Spirit intercedes for the saints in accordance with God's will" (Rom. 8:26–27).

The Holy Spirit examines our motives, teaches us what we want and need, dives into our souls and deciphers desires, suggests promises to plead, and phrases our petitions. This is hallelu praise.

R. G. Lee's unusual description of how the Holy Spirit aids in prayer has a memorable slant: "Unless the Holy

Spirit helps us, we shall be as unsuited for battle as little David with Saul's armor, as fragile against soul enemies as frozen macaroni sticks trampled on by heavy feet, as unsuccessful as the man who tried to compress a bale of cotton with a lemon squeezer."

From our vantage point, we cannot see how all the pieces of life's puzzle fit together. The Holy Spirit can see. He fights against hindrances that keep us from praying according to the will of God. To know our part, we must pray Spirit-guided prayers.

MY PART
My Cluster Has a Prayer Piece

Praise is one element of prayer consisting of three kinds of gratitude. Hallelu praise, gratitude to God for His attributes, surfaces throughout your routine. For instance, a sense of God's gentleness comforts you as you await the doctor's diagnosis. Expressing your gratitude for His gentle presence is hallelu praise.

Read the fruit of the Spirit listed in Galatians 5:22–23. Praise God for His intangible qualities that you feel are strongest in your life. Consider the weakest fruit your life exhibits. Praise God that He is faithful to help you cultivate the weak fruit.

Baracha praise is thanking God for His tangible favors. Continual prayer is possible through baracha praise as we thank God for all we touch and see. For example, you might stand in awe as the rising sun splashes the clouds strawberry mousse pink. Expressing gratitude for an occurrence in God's creation is baracha praise.

At this moment, glancing through the cabin's window, I see a red bird sitting in a yellow forsythia bush. The primary colors in nature lift my spirit. Thanking God for the bird and the bush is baracha praise.

When our house was rebuilt after a fire, the insurance adjuster suggested that we make a inventory of every room. The detailed list of furnishings and accessories would be invaluable in case of another catastrophe. The inventory became more than just a collection of items. Listing all of our possessions on pages of paper made me acutely aware of God's material blessings.

Make a inventory of the rooms in your house. Offer baracha praise for every item. Offer baracha praise for other tangible benefits that bless your life.

Hymnos praise is recognizing the Lord's all-sufficient strength through difficulties. Without hymnos praise, difficulties make us lose sight of the eternal. Through irritations and tragedies, we try to hang onto Nehemiah 8:10, "The joy of the Lord is your strength"; but sometimes the days become very gray.

Paul knew a secret in the dungeon. On the gray days happiness flees, but joy remains. The gray is not despair. It is a shadow. "I have covered you with the shadow of my hand (Isa. 51:16).

Do you every feel that your path winds through a desert? That's OK! Isaiah reminds us that the Lord has prepared a highway through the desert called the Road of Holiness. We travel home on that road with gladness, singing, and shouting for joy. Our hearts overflow with joy as the Lord enfolds us in mercy and sympathy because He has walked our path.

Confession is an element of prayer. Confession is acknowledging sin, owning up to guilt. Galatians 5:19–21 includes a list of desires and impulses of our sinful nature that form an outline for confession. Confess through these sins divided into four categories: sensual, superstitious, social, "and such like" that includes any sins not listed.

Trust the advice of Galatians 5:16 (TEV), "Let the Spirit direct your lives, and you will not satisfy the desires of the human nature."

Petition is an element of prayer requesting a benefit from God. Petitioners entreat, seek, and ask God for His help in every aspect of life.

Since our attention now is directed to God's plan to seek and to save the lost, limit your petitions to yourself as a witness. Pray for boldness to speak when tempted to be timid; inspiration to recognize the critical moment when the Holy Spirit opens an unsaved soul; appropriate words to say and Scripture to quote.

Intercession is an element of prayer pleading to God on behalf of others. I like the Latin meaning of intercession: "mediation by prayer." To intercede, we become mediators between God and people, events, or circumstances.

Intercessions are directed for others in every aspect of life. But since our attention is directed to God's plan to seek and to save the lost, limit your intercessions to lost people you meet in your routines. Ask the Holy Spirit, as He precedes you, to melt away indifference, apathy, or hostility; prepare lost hearts for the dynamite He will light in their souls; free victims from Satan's powerful grip.

When we step into the spiritual battleground of our routines, Revelation 12:11 becomes a consolation: "They overcame him by the blood of the Lamb and by the word of their testimony."

Why is prayer critical for us to do our part? Because "people do not drift toward holiness. Apart from grace-driven effort, people do not gravitate toward godliness, prayer, obedience to Scripture, faith, and delight in the Lord. We drift toward compromise and call it tolerance; we drift toward disobedience and call it freedom; we drift toward superstition and call it faith. We cherish the indiscipline of lost self-control and call it relaxation; we slouch toward prayerlessness and delude ourselves into thinking we have escaped legalism; we slide toward godlessness and convince ourselves we have been liberated."[1]

The sincere prayer we prayed last year or last week in which we committed our lives with trust and confidence to the Lord must be repeated today. Prayer to overcome hindrances to do our part must be daily. Today kneel at your altar:

NOAH
Built an altar to Jehovah
In gratitude for deliverance,
He sacrificed one of every clean
    animal and bird preserved
        in the ark.
    Noah worshiped first.

JOHN
Saw an angel offering the prayers
    of all God's people
    on a golden altar.
    John worshiped last.

Between Noah and John
    people of God
Erected altars from earth and
    unhewn stones,
Acacia and cedar wood overlaid
    with gold.
Two altars of wood covered with
    bronze and metal
Traveled with the movable, worship
    tent.

One altar was a cross, stained red,
Where life was given; atonement made.

What is an altar?
A velvet kneeling bench?
A table displaying worship symbols?
An elaborate platform in a cathedral?
   Altar is a harsh word.
Altar means "to slaughter."
On an altar formed from the moments
of every day, I will slaughter self.
In my "altared" life, Jesus Christ
"who loved me and in his grace gives me unfailing
courage and a firm hope will encourage and strengthen
me to always do and say what is good" (2 Thess. 2:16)

[1]D. A. Carson, "Quoted," *Advance,* October 22, 2000 [newsletter
online]; available from www.brigada.org; Internet.

CONCLUSION

"Your kingdom come" (Matt. 6:10).

As we assembled "Tempting Sweets," every now and then we pointed to the same empty space in the puzzle and questioned, "Why can't we find this piece? Has anyone seen a shape to fit here?" We searched for the piece under the table and behind cushions. Since all of us enjoy placing with a flourish the last piece in a puzzle, we accused each other of hiding one piece of "Tempting Sweets."

Finally, in the 1,000-piece puzzle, 999 shapes interlocked. One piece was missing. The intrusion of the green table top beneath the space for that piece lured our attention away from the other 999 pieces forming the fabulous chocolates. The missing piece became the most important part of "Tempting Sweets."

We ended our work on the puzzle, but we did not complete the picture.

PUZZLE PIECE
Imagine the Globe Puzzle with a Missing Piece

The Book of Acts ends abruptly. Luke's history of the Holy Spirit leading believers to spread Christianity does not end with a dynamic revival, a dramatic scene before the emperor, or the martyrdom of Paul. Acts ends as it began—talking about Jesus and His kingdom (Acts 1:1–7; 28:31).

During Jesus' ministry, even His most ardent followers shared the notion that Jesus would establish a political kingdom. On numerous occasions, Jesus talked about the kingdom of heaven (Matt. 13:1–53). However, the disciples, and even John the Baptist who had preached the kingdom of heaven (Matt. 3:2), misinterpreted His teachings.

For people unfamiliar with a reigning monarch, the idea of kingdom is difficult to grasp. To help people understand His kingdom, Jesus might have borrowed a situation from the Roman Empire. Rome was the magnificent government, social, and cultural center of the world; but scattered over the enormous empire were colonies identical to Rome in architecture and the layout of the streets, in customs and fashions, in politics and religion. The colonies were not temporary frontier posts. Each one was a miniature Rome. To reside in a colony was an honor.

When Jesus requested of God, "Your kingdom come," He not only envisioned a future kingdom where God will reign but also He pictured the Spirit of God in redeemed believers—colonies spread over the world.

Paul emphasized this reality in 2 Corinthians 6:16–18 and in 1 Corinthians 3:16: "Don't you know that you yourselves are God's temple and God's Spirit lives in you?" Paul described the attributes of the kingdom: "For the kingdom of God is not a matter of eating and drinking, but of righteousness, peace and joy in the Holy Spirit" (Rom. 14:17).

When God resides in us, He establishes a bit of His kingdom within us. At this moment we individually exemplify kingdom life: God decides our affairs. His righteousness accepts or alters our attitudes and directs or redirects our affairs. His peace is a deep soul serenity in spite of trouble or persecutions. His joy is a quiet confidence in His control. His righteousness, peace, and joy free us from fear no matter how tempestuous life's circumstances may be or where life situations will scatter us. When we pray, "Your kingdom come," we invite God to become paramount in our lives. What an honor!

Acts 28:31 summarizes Paul's ministry: "Boldly and without hindrance he preached the kingdom of God and taught about the Lord Jesus Christ." Paul died. His martyrdom finished his physical part in God's plan. But the plan remained incomplete. God's plan to seek and to save the lost continued. Believers in every generation preached the "kingdom of God and taught about the Lord Jesus Christ."

The missing piece in the globe puzzle illustrates that the message of grace has not reached everyone. The plan progresses through my part believing the promise, "The plans of the Lord stand firm forever, the purposes of his heart through all generations" (Psalm 33:11). The plan moved forward through my part, encouraged by Paul's cheer, "Being confident of this, that he who began a good work in you will carry it on to completion until the day of Christ Jesus" (Phil. 1:6).

Until Jesus returns with His kingdom intact, there is no end to sharing God's grace, only a succession of beginnings.

MY PART
My Cluster Has a Name—Pièce de Résistance

The word ensemble of *Plan, Part,* and *Part and Parcel* contains another concept: *pièce de résistance.* When used in

English conversation, the phrase can mean "important person."

Do you realize how special you are to God? When He looked at His Son dying on a cross, He saw you dying with Him. God considers you the pièce de résistance on the street where you live. Sharing the message of grace will eliminate missing pieces in your sphere of influence.

My part in God's plan is not a response to an austere summons. It is a victorious venture of limitless possibilities and promise.

Pièce de résistance, rejoice in God's plan for you, "plans to prosper you and not to harm you, plans to give you hope and a future (Jer. 29:11).